HOW TEACHERS

TEACHER

LEARN TO USE MINECRAFT

CRAFT

IN THEIR CLASSROOMS

BY SEANN DIKKERS

TABLE OF CONTENTS

ACKNOWLEDGEMENTS

The entirety of this book has had the contribution of an active and entirely helpful community of Minecraft using teachers. This is so much so, that credit should be shared. Not only does this book have some phenomenal guest authors writing, but I have had core community members that have been willing to vet chapters, provide feedback, and generally keep me in balance when presenting this world to you.

Thanks also to you, for picking up the book/PDF. Thanks for your encouragement, interest, for using it in your classes, giving it as a gift to a teacher you know, and caring about what expert teachers are doing with their skills and talents. Your interest in this topic, and Minecraft, is a credit to our profession and the passion that we have to make better experiences for learners. Thank you.

My wife and two children have been active product testers, experts, and editors of this book. Every chapter had to be approved by my Minecraft family. They are my inspiration and teachers at home, and most of what I know about Minecraft started with and is checked against their expertise.

In addition, there are the Minecraft people that were both subjects for the study, but some also became pointed critics/supporters/readers of this work. They have entrusted me with their outstanding stories and I am seeking to present their ideas as they would have them read. I've come to a deep respect for the genius that is collectively being refined by this community. Special thanks are reserved for Zack Gilbert, Steven Isaacs, Joel Levin, Mark Suter, Peggy Sheehy, Donelle Batty, and Andrew Peterson for conversations, readings, and guiding the tone, content, and claims of this book. Finally, the Chapter 10 team of Joseph C. Toscano, Andrés Buxó-Lugo, and Duane G. Watson and their contribution of a chapter that shows off research use of Minecraft.

I want to thank the supportive and engaging community of scholars in the Patton College of Education at Ohio University. I thank Drs. Moore, Byrne, Machtmes, Robinson, Henning, Paulins, and Kessler for their brilliant thinking, leadership, friendship and conversations around games for learning. Finally, Drs. Lucas and Saunders who were partners in co-building the *Athens Makers* club where we were able to play test Minecraft with a group of incredible students for ourselves. Thanks for getting your hands dirty with me. This book relied on your help.

Nothing happens, in my world, without a team of generous and alive graduate students that free up the time to write. On this particular project credit needs to be given to a few that helped specifically to edit manuscript, contribute ideas, or even just help me get blocks of time free by handling other projects with expertise. Thank you especially to Donelle Batty for traveling across the world to help with this project, Jeff Kuhn and Mike Cisneros for writing, and Mark Mace for his digital contributions and help.

This study was first conceived in the GLS community at the University of Wisconsin-Madison and under the constructivist advising of Drs. Kurt Squire and Richard Halverson. I appreciate their encouragement, permission, and especially their vision. My passion for identifying expert teaching practices was born out of their gifted work and research along with others at UW. I also appreciate the ongoing guidance of Drs. Kelley, Camburn, Steinkuehler, and Erica Halverson while spending the last five years learning from their scholarship skills, superpowers, and their Teachercraft.

TEACHERCRAFT?

"We are currently at 4.85 million registered users and then out of those users, 8.1 million have purchased the game on PC and Mac platforms. We also have 5 million purchases on mobile devices, ios, android and amazon. We have 3.5 million copies sold on the xBox."

- Carl Manneh[1], Mojang | Co-founder and Managing Director

Minecraft for Learning

Minecraft[2] was released as a beta with little fanfare initially. With a dedicated and active fanbase it has grown into one of the most successful games on the market. Uniquely, Minecraft offers a space that can be infinitely recreated using a simple 'block' model interface in servers that users set up to play with friends. Minecraft is both a game and a tool for creation with your friends. Surrounding the game are a number of user-created modifications, forums, and communities that share, critique, and build new challenges for themselves. Minecraft is more than a game, it is a hobby and a community.

It is also getting used increasingly in classroom settings.

Like a blank sheet of paper and a box of crayons can be used for learning, Minecraft is begging creators to make any 3D object, building, or idea they can think of. It is a creation-media that is, and has been, quickly adopted and used in learning settings all over the world. Minecraft can serve teachers in the same way that a sheet of paper, a canvas, or a pile of building blocks can facilitate learner representations of understanding across topics, age levels, and learner ability. Interestingly, some early adopting teachers have been doing exactly that. They are using Minecraft for learning.

This book is built around a set of teacher interviews that describe the practices and perceptions of educators as they are adopting, modifying, and building learning environments that integrate Minecraft. They see Minecraft as an essential learning tool in

---

[1] Interview with Carl Manneh on December 4, 2012.

[2] Copyrighted by Mojang. For readability, I will not insert © throughout the book.

both formal and informal learning environments. So this book is an effort to provide context, description, evaluation, and common threads across the interviews of teachers using Minecraft. More than a list of ideas, I am attempting to provide a rich description of how these teachers think about practice, the kinds of things they see when they look at an active classroom, and what matters to their crafting of lessons, their 'Teachercraft'.

Teachercraft is unique to the use of Minecraft in this book, but is not isolated. It has implications for the use of any digitally mediated learning space, the adoption of technology for learning, and more broadly a picture of how teachers learn. Using a tool like Minecraft for learning is clearly innovative teaching. I wonder how these teachers go about learning new ideas? Where did they find out about Minecraft? How do they gain knowledge of new software and validate its use for learning? How did teachers test new ideas? Appropriate Minecraft? What did they actually do with Minecraft in class? And how did they evaluate the effectiveness of Minecraft, as a digital experience within actual classroom expectations? These questions are at the core of this book and assume that teachers have relevant insights to share about how teachers go about innovative thinking, learning, and practical application.

Chapter Overview

Each following chapter answers a question related to Teachercraft. First, for context, I start Chapter 1 with a brief overview of 'Why Games?' are being used in classrooms for teaching and learning. What kind of learning game proponents are advocating for and what kinds of proposals are compelling when discussing the use of games for learning.

In Chapter 2, I'll provide an overview of 'Why Minecraft?' and present possible reasons why so many have chosen to place special attention on this game. Minecraft has four unique play goals that make it a benchmark learning product as the media matures: production, creative thinking, safe/limited social play, and modding. These four traits, in combination, provide teachers a unique classroom product that can be adopted to any subject or age level for a variety of applications, assignments, and amplifications of subject area learning.

But, Minecraft is first a game! Millions of players have booted up for fun, not school. So in Chapter 3, we will welcome Mike Cisneros, as my guide answering, "How do I Start Playing?" and hope that this will encourage any non-players to play before reading on. He provides a unique and charming insider's perspective to booting up, playing, and having fun with Minecraft; and even as a college student, he has a masterful and helpful touch in helping future builders.

Chapter 4 provides a short overview of the qualitative study this book is associated with. The chapter starts with a theoretical approach to understanding teachers that leads to this kind of study. That said, I have taken care to make this justification as readable as possible for the non-academic audience, because it has very real implications for teacher professional development and training programs. The second half of the chapter explains the methods used for the interviews. These foundations of research for interviewing Minecraft teachers establishes the reliability and relevance of the rest of the stories in the book. Chapter 4 provides a glimpse of the cooperating teachers, how they were selected, who they are, and what context they are teaching within.

Chapters 5 through 9 will answer questions about Teachercraft. Chapter 5 asks how these teachers validate the use of Minecraft, or more broadly, any new digital technology, for their classrooms. This process of validation looks diverse, complex, and far more robust than simple approval of a new idea.

Chapter 6 explains a common validation approach for teachers that tried out their new ideas after school or in a 'club' before bringing Minecraft into classroom settings. This 'petri dish' examination is fleshed out with stories from the teachers about how they used the time for their own learning, tried out new designs, and finally, guest author Zack Gilbert gives a very practical guide for building your own gaming club.

Chapter 7 focuses on classroom lesson ideas used by teachers. More than just the ideas, however, teachers share their philosophy of learning, pedagogical strategies, and types of lessons that are applicable across subject and age levels. In the second half of the chapter, I attempt to sort additional lessons into subject specific ideas.

After seeing how teachers used Minecraft, Chapter 8 attempts to provide an insider's approach to evaluating whether or not those lessons were effective. I'm interested here in how using new mediums for learning has an affect on what measures are relevant to these teachers. What tools and approaches do they use to evaluate the tool, the lesson idea, and how can Minecraft be used as an evaluation tool?

Chapter 9 shows how Minecraft teachers used outside resources for classroom use. Minecraft alone, or 'vanilla Minecraft', is just the beginning for experienced Teachercrafting. Once they become familiar with the basic tool, students and teachers start to create new 'skins', 'seeds', 'maps', and 'servers' to meet particular classroom needs and further lesson ideas.

In Chapter 10, I welcome guest authors who have been using Minecraft as a research tool. While I understand that 'research tools' are not necessarily for classrooms, I think this chapter has much greater reach and shows how teaching and learning extends beyond the K-12 classroom too. The tone and pace of the book will be a bit more formal here, but I hope you find this as truly impressive and innovative as our research team did when we invited them to participate in the book.

All of these discussions together flesh out what the use of Minecraft for learning looks like in practice. This is interesting, with many, many more digital tools coming our way, to see what effective teaching with digital tools looks like; and it can inform how we practice, train new teachers, and support innovative teaching today. With so much to cover, we start with building a strong argument for using games like Minecraft in the classroom.

CHAPTER 1

WHY GAMES?

"We took a little time to think what could we do with
this and how could we use it..."

- Minecraft Teacher

Kids These Days!

Kids these days are playing a lot of video games. Popular videogames are not just for fun, many academics are growing enthusiastic about the potential and early results of using games for learning. In this book we look at a particular game that entertains millions of players. Minecraft has a growing fan base and teachers are quickly imagining ways it can be used for learning.

Yet other writers are not as impressed with these games. They ask why we should embrace a hobby for the 'serious' work of education. You may have already heard some form of these published sentiments:

> Games are just a waste of time?[1]
> Games are violent and anti-social?[2]
> Students should instead be quiet, sit down, and study the [heck] out of things?[3]

In fact, after ten years of more than promising research and evidence that games can be good for learning, these questions are still clearly espoused by prominent thinkers.

Why is this the case? Why do some still challenge the idea that millions of video game players claim they are getting value out of their game time? 'Worth' is a relative idea. Why do some still critique gaming? I will suggest that it is because gaming media is still growing and we have not yet seen their place in education.

Kids 'these days' are a lot like those of past generations. Without years of training toward a particular channel of media, youth are drawn to forms of media that allow them to learn from others. Youth have historically led the way in legitimizing new media as they grow into adults. Today, they are playing digital video games en masse. Today, many are saying that games provide exceptional experiences, stories, challenges, and social engagement. So, why do we doubt the entertainment media of an entire generation?

Are Books Bad?

Consider how Plato disdained the "new" media of books:

> "If men learn this, it will implant forgetfulness in their souls; they will cease to exercise memory because they rely on that which is written, calling things to remembrance no longer from within themselves, but by means of external marks. What you have discovered is a recipe not for memory, but for reminder. And it is no true wisdom that you offer your disciples... for the most part they know nothing, and as men filled, not with wisdom, but with the conceit of wisdom, they will be a burden to their fellows."

Plato believed that memory was central to all teaching and learning. Notice he equates memorizing words to wisdom itself! For one of the world's most accomplished memorizers Plato could see the growing popularity of written texts - and even added his memoized teachings of Socrates to the ancient works! Yet he valued Socrates wisdom as higher than that contained in the book.

Plato felt books were shortcuts to the "hard labors" of real learning. Real learning was to put in the time with your teacher to memorize their every word. Oral traditions have interculturally shown to be stunningly accurate and generationally consistent because of the societal value placed on scribes and scholars that recorded and committed to memory many of the great works of history. This took considerable effort that reading could potentially delay and make lazy learners that wouldn't sustain high levels of learning - or worse, be "a burden" to society.

Plato saw a great loss in reading because it is a *one way*, second-hand, interaction. Reading is impersonal. If the reader does not understand, the written word continues on. The writer cannot elaborate if needed, nor can they read facial expressions, crowd response, learn from choice of words. The reader cannot ask questions, understand tonal qualities of the speaker, pick up on facial expressions, or see others in the audience reacting to the speaker. Reading is essentially anti-social.

Reading allows the writer to share violent acts, lurid drama, and emotive content without the accountability of a crowd (and nearby stones to throw). Reading can, therefore, be violent and lead to violent thoughts! Meaning and ethical considerations could be part of these narratives, but without a teacher on hand, reading had the potential to be misunderstood. Reading pretends to be meaningful without the attention or moral considerations that memorization requires.

Yet, despite these valid concerns, the overwhelming historical result of reading media has been a more educated citizenry. Plato wrote his teacher Socrates' words; a generation later, Aristotle wrote his own words, and we were never the same. Books did not eliminate the value or potency of an outstanding lecture, nor have they replaced public speaking as a media. Instead teachers began to perceive and use books to great benefit - adding multiple tools for learning.

Media Channels

Negative expectations arise from fear of losing something personally valued. Plato was not wrong to doubt the future of memorized words, but he was mistaken in thinking that memorizing words heard in-person are the only way to learn. In fact humans have learned that we have multiple senses, multiple learning preferences, and there are multiple channels that media forms can use to educate. Plato couldn't conceive of a high quality of education occurring with books as the central media in the lesson plan, but in retrospect this is not hard to see for us.

Today we get 'lost' in books, we lose track of time reading, we even 'forget' ourselves in the written thoughts of another. The best writers have found a way to effectively convey tone, clarity, and voice in their writing. We fill bookstores, and Kindles, full of books because they are fun, engaging, and we learn from them.

Many teachers use written texts as the center of their lesson planning and design because they aren't entirely bad for kids. Teachers also have found ways to make use of books as learning media. They have written their own genre of 'text' books, and adopted assignments focused on writing so that learners can build their capacity to produce valuable contributions of their own. New media, like text, has historically added to our options in education, rather than competing with or eliminating other media.

Media channels are value neutral. The 'channels' through which we receive media encourage personal preference (like Plato's oral learning), and we hone our literacies for learning based on the media channels we prefer. Readers get better at reading, viewers get better at viewing, and speakers get better at speaking. Expert readers may not have a tendency to value movie watching, but this preference should never be interpreted as actual value. Media value is in the effectiveness with which it communicates, entertains, informs, and engages the reader.

Books are not essentially bad - they are a form of media. They are a particular channel for information and ideas to travel through. Those ideas however carry with them a worldview and perspectives that are laden with value. Value is embedded in the message that is communicated through media. Our question for books, and all media channels, should be the extent to which they can reach people with a message or experience. In that sense, games are clearly a powerful media channel.

Despite any loss of memorized content, anti-social tendencies, and moral ambiguity, books are generally considered an educational asset. Books have the benefits of mass production, permanence, and have developed common formats. For all the books that have been burned, others have elevated the human condition. The mass production of the written word has arguably transformed institutions, nations, contractual relationships, and power holders - toward a more democratized and equitable world.

Games will do the same.

What if we could have looked inside the classrooms of those Greek teachers that Plato was complaining about? What were they doing differently? How were they forming daily decisions to make use of these books? What we could learn from those book reading Greeks and Romans?

As a former history teacher, I would *love* to go back in time to see early innovators using books! One look at those early adopters would show both the early mistakes and the early seeds of change toward a new way to think about teaching and learning - that would lead to 'readers', 'textbooks', and 'syllabi' as teacher adoptions of books for learning. 'Today, we are at that point of inception for digital tools and resources for the classroom. How they will eventually be used will be born out of how teachers use them and dream of using them now.

Digital gaming is capturing the attention of kids today. Elders are scoffing at it, but as a media channel, it can tell powerful stories, challenge the mind, and convey the thinking of designers. Gaming media is proliferating as the media of choice and I want to know much, much more about what teachers are doing to adopt and use gaming in their classrooms.

Games for Learning

Teacher adoption of new media has determined the degree to which it gets used in the learning process. Many schools have libraries built into them today. In addition, libraries have added books, music, video, and audio collections. Yet, however stocked the libraries are, the teacher gets to decide how media gets used for close to thirty-seven million public school students for six hours or more each day.

Games for learning is a logical development. If games are a powerful media channel, it star to reason that some of those games can be effective and powerful learning experiences. ¯ question is, how do we better see the future of games for learning in the classroom? do we explain and move forward with better educational designs, better game design actual use of games for learning?

Teacher-experts matter. We need to keep an eye on the teacher-innovators that are e' around games for learning. This book is dedicated to only a small number of thes

We need more. Expert teachers are the first, best, and by sheer force of numbers, the most likely place that we will find seeds of transformative educational practices. This starts with valuing their role as an expert audience for games for learning - and as expert learning designers.

Rhetoric matters. We cannot further confuse the discussion of games for learning with poor rhetorical constructs (bad arguments). Moving past, or addressing, the negative arguments above is a collective task for advocates of games for learning. In addition, I'll share dogmatic arguments coming from games for learning advocates. We need balanced and logically consistent arguments that have the potential to move game and classroom design forward.

Gaming matters. Finally, we need to continue to build a positive understanding of what effective gaming media looks like from an educational perspective. When educators begin to design, they start with learning goals, and gaming media choices will be made based on the games potential to meet those goals. Below I'll suggest a framework to define and discern effective gaming media from ineffective designs. Educators should demand better games and know what to ask for.

These three lenses provide context for conversation that you may have when you talk to an administrator, parents, or even explain to students why you are going to boot up Minecraft. At the very least, these provide context for why myself and the other writers in this book have chosen Minecraft adoption as a focus for this study. Teachers, rhetoric, and gaming itself are of value to the entire field and we see their learning potential as nothing short of what Plato's books offered humanity years ago.

Teacher-Experts Matter

First, teachers are experts. Least lets start with the assumption that teachers are excellent at their jobs. They are also very, very busy experts. They have to design, teach, and iterate lessons for kids on a scale and pace that is hard for non-educators to understand. But, it's important that we do understand and respect their expertise in the politicized atmosphere that we hear on the news.

For instance, for every singular lesson design that a researcher tests; a teacher prepares a lesson that gets tested in practice with up to 180 kids in 3-6 iterations (classes) per day (180/year). For the average high school teacher, with five classes (n=@30), that amounts to around 27,000 student reactions to lessons - per year. After one year of teaching, most teachers will have an experienced feel for whether or not a lesson plan will work well and with which types of learners it will work.

By the time that teacher is up for tenure (usually three years), they may have tested lesson ideas, in actual practice, over 4500 times. If that teacher has generally reported to work each day they will have easily garnered over 10,000 hours, (Gladwell's suggested condition for expertise)[4], of time designing and delivering learning experiences to youth. Regardless of their availability to write this experience in a peer reviewed journal, most teachers have an expertise that is deeply rooted in their work with learners.

If teachers can become experienced in their practice simply because of time on task - even mediocre ones - they should have a respectable baloney detector for non-educators telling them how to change their lesson planning. This doesn't necessarily make them skeptics, (as outsiders often mistake this as), but it does make them a seasoned and salty population.

I've found that what can feel like a fight from teachers is actually a form of testing to see if an idea can hold it's own in the world of practice. If it does, I've yet to meet a teacher that isn't willing to try something that they see as a *better* way of teaching than their current methods. We need not waste time 'convincing' teachers, but invest more effort in *showing* them learning methods that surpass current practices.

This speaks to educational change. Teachers are commonly being blamed for 'out-dated' practices. This is easy, but not productive. Nor will perceived teacher resistance (like Plato) matter much as we move forward. If we have media options that effectively educate youth with new ideas and abilities, demand and time will have it's way as early adopters figure out what learning will look like in practice. Speeding up reform efforts will happen as we *show* this expert audience what might be done better and allow them their professional expertise to play with, refine, and develop learning plans that integrate new media.

Here we offer up Minecraft as a potential teaching resource. Instead of mandating that all teachers use Minecraft, lets start by looking at those experts that have already used it and plan to continue using it as a classroom tool. Some of these teachers have utilized this game to become the central learning activity in the classroom supplemented by a host of existing pedagogical practices. We should listen first.

Then we should help to communicate examples of practice with sound rationale and understanding. Any argument that suggests change, to those working in arguably the world's most effective educational system ever, should be convincing. We need to present these examples with reasonable and well balanced logic. If not, these master practitioners will kick back with some salty questions and calmly go about preparing their next lesson using their well established methods.

Rhetoric Matters

If you have never enjoyed the pleasure of martial arts films, you have missed out on the popcorn version of "Kung Fu". In the movies, Kung Fu isn't bad or good, it's just a measure of having 'form'. Out of balance combatants have 'weak Kung Fu' and those in balance have 'strong kung fu'. The difference is not the moral stance of the character, it's the balance that they have and their ability to retain that balance under stress. Argumentation, or rhetorical design, is similar.

Rhetoric, in the classical sense is the "art that aims to improve the capability of speakers that attempt to inform, persuade, or motivate particular audiences..."[5] Rhetoric requires a form that is both designed by the speaker and in response to an audience - it requires balance. The central goal is not to argue, but to, in the end, agree. I even like the ordering of informing first, then persuading, then motivating action. Sadly, this process takes time and patience (like strong Kung Fu!), and mandating action is often easier than rhetorically constructing consensus across a population.

Strong Kung Fu is usually found in those with physical, mental, and spiritual balance - at least in the movies. Balance requires a certain calm, awareness of the context, and understanding of your challenge. Weak Kung Fu is found in the young, the rash, and usually the over-reaching pride found in the villian. (This is usually shown in a 5-minute training montage showing the hero growing stronger both physically, mentally, and spiritually.) The hero grows from weak Kung Fu to stronger Kung Fu and this usually has something to do with hard work, humility, and appreciation for expertise.

The cumulative lesson (from a childhood of watching bad captions) is that balanced rhetoric is more important than force of will or excitement around a topic. The alternatives are exaggerated and fanatical statements like "All games are good!" or "Games cause violence!"; neither is strong Kung Fu. As educational leaders, it is not our job to cheerlead, or worse, to mandate; its our job to inform, persuade, and motivate.

Weak Kung Fu

In this book, we suggest that games are good for learning, but some arguments for this are more balanced than others. You should avoid weak arguments not because they are necessarily wrong, but because they present an off-balance logic that is easy to redirect into unnecessary debates.

Strong Kung Fu avoids conflict when possible and manages it when necessary. Lets first look at weak Kung Fu examples, then start training for better rhetoric. I propose that some of the outlying resistance to games for learning actually comes from those that are seeking to promote games.

Consider these very popular arguments:

1) Games are popular with kids...
2) No, games are *really* popular with all ages...
3) Games require *learning* a game to play and master...
4) Games are really *complex* systems...
5) Games make complex learning *fun!*

Depending on your audience, you may actually use and believe all of these premises to be accurate. I'll admit to using them myself. Yet they didn't always lead to the responses that I was hoping for. In fact, more often than not, these lead to skepticism and counter-kicks from teachers. Why?

For a moment review the above list and replace "games" with "books" and ask if the arguments would be compelling - even for an established media.

Learning in general is of course a fascinating topic, but formal schooling currently happens within an established state centric system that demands learning *outcomes*. Those outcomes are predominantly defined, and effectively tested, as the ability to 1) read non-fiction texts, and 2) solve decontextualized math problems quickly. Other standards exist, and more tests are being designed. That system may be in contest with other options, but the public school model still houses most of our students. We have a content driven system.

Teachers are asked to teach specific content that has been agreed to be 'relevant' by the state, school boards, and indirectly by parents that choose your school for their kids. Today they have actual, written, standards that they are accountable to teach. For this reason, teachers are on the lookout not just for any learning experiences, but *those that meet the classroom objectives of teachers.*

With that in mind, review each of the questions above and ask (as many teachers do), how does this help me teach my content? Fill in the blank and try it a few times with each question: Chemistry? Adverbs? The American Revolution? Long division? Do you see the disconnect? Like Plato, it's hard to see a future where learning facts is not central to the learning model.

Any media might be popular, require learning, be complex, or provide amazing fun, but they may not be what teachers consider 'classroom' learning. On the flip side, not all game designs are actually well described as popular, complex, learning rich, or fun.

Some games just aren't up to a level of quality where they represent the findings in the research community. So 'games' and 'learning' can be unique and non-associated variables; games are a media channel, and learning is a value that can be gained, or not. Not all games, (or any media type), are good for classroom experiences and it follows that not all games will motivate teachers to try them out in class.

Strong Kung Fu

While all games may or may not be popular, learning rich, complex, or fun, consider that some games have been exactly that. On the flip side, while all games are not necessarily good for classroom learning, some games have been shown to be exactly that. Consider rhetoric that allows for deviants. When we cease making sweeping claims about 'games', we can start to speak to our common concern for learning and kids. Using the same arguments with more balanced rhetoric, and connecting the media to learning as a measure, our presentation dramatically improves:

1) *Some* games are 'popular' with the kids and learning can be more engaging by tying into student interest areas.

2) Some games require intense learning, and some games provide learning experiences pertinent to classroom use.

3) Games have varying degrees of complexity and some are uniquely able to present experiences that are in line with classroom learning objectives.

4) Schools aren't necessarily fun, (nor do educators have an obligation to make them fun), but they are more tolerable, engaging, social, and functional when fun can be integrated into learning.

Consider how these claims both 1) represent accurate logic, and 2) direct the conversants to consider the individual game, not the entire media type. Why make sweeping claims when specific, balanced, Kung Fu will do? Some games are great experiences, and this book is full of examples that Minecraft is one of those.

Gaming, as a whole, does not have to be defended in order to justify use in the classroom. We do *not* have to claim a universal attribute for *all* games in order to claim that the attribute exists for a *particular* game that we intend to use for a purpose. For instance, we don't have to claim that all books are valuable to teachers, only that *this* book is relevant for a classroom.

Strong rhetoric helps to avoid massive and irrelevant discussions about whether or not games are a waste of time, causes violence, or if you are dumbing down the curriculum. For instance if asked, "Don't games make kids think about poking people?", consider the balance in saying, "Perhaps, I'm not aware of any studies on *Minecraft* that show increased poking. I have read about teachers that use Minecraft to teach science." Games, therefore, are not necessarily even pertinent for classroom teachers... but in chapter two I'll lay out exactly why Minecraft is.

My own musings on balanced Kung Fu, shouldn't be read as an excuse to gloss over well done research either - even when it makes larger claims. Schools that are interested in the best possible delivery of relevant curriculum should strongly consider that some games have *proven track records* of being engaging, intelligent, complex, and rigorous learning media with iterations that are useful across age and subject areas.

Gaming is an emerging media format with great promise for teaching and learning. Models of games for learning are beginning to proliferate and great teachers make it their work to know what and how to engage kids with learning experiences that work in their classrooms. They know that gaming is relevant, useful, and powerful when designed well.

Gaming Matters

Scholar Larry Cuban reminds us, repeatedly, that radio and television did little to transform the American classroom.[6] More recently Larry Cuban argues compellingly that the 'digital revolution' isn't all that revolutionary.[7] Personally, I imagine Dr. Cuban reading a claim that, 'Games can be powerful learning tools!', and shrugging. Exciting technology that appears very revolutionary can, and often does, end up having much less impact on classrooms than we thought. What if games are a fad?

I'm motivated to introduce Minecraft in the next chapter, but first convince my 'Imaginary Larry' that it's worth taking a look at games as a learning space as a distinct media channel.

At the very least, the teachers represented in this study present a series of revolutionized Minecraft classrooms, even if on a small scale. For them, gaming matters because of their experience with learners. This same population of teachers, that are not as impressed with television, report that games are different from other media.

There are some considerations about games that support their relevance for learning above and beyond more established media. Before moving on to Minecraft, we will consider that games can be viewed developmentally, both inside and outside of formal learning spaces, where consumption and production are closely partnered, and as a 'lean forward' media.

Big Red Developmental Dogs

Today, there is little disagreement that when kids read books, they are developing a skill or proficiency that will help them read other books. Less prevalent is that kids music also matures into pop music and adult preference. Kids movies graduate to adult themes and topics. So even, if for now, kids are reading Clifford books, we naturally expect them to later read novels, news, and professional texts.

Elementary school libraries are filled with books that are fun, silly, playful, and appeal to young readers. We know that it is *the capacity to read,* and read with understanding, that is our accepted goal for children learning a media. As books lead to familiarity with the printed word, I am interested as games providing the same kind of familiarity with digital content.

Not every game should be evaluated for it's specific learning outcomes, but for their ability to attract and engage youth toward digital content. For established media, we excuse 'childish content' because we value the adult ability to be proficient with the media. If we value the ability to communicate, 'read', and quickly navigate digital spaces, we need to do the same for gaming media.

Do we allow the same understanding of the value of games like *Windosill, Williamspurrg,* or *Clash of Clans*? This is perhaps what Plato was unable to see from his perspective. He only saw the popularity of Greek drama, (which, let's be honest, wasn't Shakespeare...), and Plato made judgements about popular forms of the media without full understanding of mature or educationally designed forms of that media.

Consider the mature narrative power of *Mass Effect*, the calming effect of Flower, or the historical accuracy of *Assassin's Creed* cities, or the graphic wonder (art) of *Elder Scrolls Online*. Are these being similarly overlooked by critics? These are exactly the things that adult gamers discuss and are amazed by.

In the same way that we allow "Reading Time" to elementary readers, (or at least we should!), I advocate for similar "Gaming Time" that includes playful and compelling games, libraries full of fun and delightful games. We would see children's media evolve and benefit from feedback from educators that track what media is consumed, improved proficiency with the basic tools of our society, and hopefully could expect gaming interests to mature too.

The media of gaming represents a spectrum of complexity that leads not to topical content necessarily, but to a *proficiency* with digital media, digital communications, and digital communities. Games, like books, have a range of 'reading levels'; and Clifford games should progressively lead to much more compelling forms of media, and eventually to digital 'reading' skills that will help youth in the workplace.

Gaming Outside the Classroom

We have long accepted that the *habit of learning*[8] toward a subject is as relevant as the information that we expect to later be consumed through that media channel. The media of a book is a 'must learn' even when simpler forms include a big red dog, young sleuths, aliens, or parties of adventurers. For this reason educators have long encouraged learning outside of the school day through reading programs, summer clubs, after school programming, and strong communication with the home.

This isn't complex: If kids read for fun, they will be better readers. If we value proficiency with computers, we can safely assume that if kids play with computers for fun, they will likewise be better at learning and 'reading' software. The variables are guidance, availability, and encouragement to all children.

In our past book, *Mobile Media Learning*[9] I guided chapter authors to consider questions from Dewey's *Democracy in Education*[10] when reviewing their experiments designing mobile games for learning. Dewey considered an education that allowed each student to construct their understanding of the world through experiences. So when games are employed outside of classroom settings, we should consider this as a natural fit for an experiential media.

This study finds that teachers are using Minecraft to build experiences (as true classroom grandmasters) in a way that fulfills the theoretical expectations of Dewey. Not all of them rely on minutes allocated during the school day. Educators consider the whole child and respect that if they engage with content for fun, they will be better learners.

Yes, games do take time. Some games take large amounts of time, but we shouldn't be skeptical based on time because we see teachers creatively encouraging play outside of traditional class times. If media can transform learning, like it did for Plato, we should expect that context, time, and teacher-student relationships may also transform.

Producing Ideas

One filter to understand new technology, and the veracity of a 'digital revolution', is to ask if the technology helps humans to be receivers of ideas, or to be producers of ideas. While some get excited about the potential and power of new tools alone (the Industrial Revolution!), some wait for the tools of production to be put into the hands of the masses (Communism!... err... 3D Printing!).

Technology has the power to transform - it's just a matter of seeing how things will pan out and to what degree the ability of production will be left to people. Gaming is uniquely enabled by the exact same instruments that allow for its production. Though some delivery tools block off a range creation tools (console gaming), others allow games and game production tools to exist on the same toolbar.

It is because games allow learners to use digital tools, provide experiences, are increasingly cooperative, and because they can often address very specific classroom learning needs that they should be part of a suite of learning tools at a teacher's disposal.

Games, *like any other media*, are subject to the skill of the teacher that uses them. Quality teaching is still at the center of classroom learning environments. Games can be used badly in a classroom, adopted for poor learning goals, or applied without clear mentoring, frameworks, or purpose. This is not unique to gaming media. The goal is to seek a balance that avoids poor pedagogical approaches and leverages powerful learning opportunities.

Specifically, teaching and learning, is best when teachers create clear objectives, guidance for mastering them, and ask students to be responsible for the production and representation of them. Ultimately teachers in this study each appropriate Minecraft as a learning tool to be bended to their own philosophy of teaching and learning.

This is why teachers don't want products that teach for them (packaged content), they want component tools they can *use* in new ways to communicate, share, and interact with learners (editable content). The more we push standards, develop prescription curriculums, and worry about 'fidelity of practice' between teachers and content specialists, the more teachers should push back.

In a healthy learning setting teachers are reacting to students with a clear set of objectives for the learning and using a variety of tools to engage and challenge learners. Teachers don't want a better production, they want to *broadcast*. It's not about finding the right game, it's about allowing teachers to find the right game. We will see that Minecraft teachers like Minecraft because it allows them to teach, it doesn't tell them how.

Leaning backward and forward

When it comes to games, educators often recoil at the thought of students playing computer games all day, but to ask students to design and make a computer game has much more allure. Teaching and learning, at their best, are 'lean forward', not lean backward' activities. This explains some resistance to gaming for learning, but also provides insights on the implementation of games as an educational media.

Lean Backward Media and Lean Forward Production have manifestations in every technology for learning, across media types:

Lean Backward and Lean Forward Technologies

LEAN BACKWARD MEDIA	LEAN FORWARD PRODUCTION
Listen to a story	Tell a story
Financial receipts	Running a trading coster
Reading the Iliad	Writing the Odyssey
Visiting the Louvre	Finger painting
Listening to Green Hornet radio	Recording War of the 'Worldlies'
Watching the Muppet Show	Putting on a puppet show
Watching Star Wars	Making an indy film
Cheering	Scoring
Buying stuff	Making stuff
Cutscenes in a computer game	Playing a computer game

Both applications can be educational, but clearly leaning forward creates greater potential for student engagement with the content. There are already some outstanding books that dedicate all of their pages to why games are powerful options for teaching and learning and I encourage reading those to prepare for discussions about games.

For our purposes, presenting games for learning can be as simple as,

1) Games don't replace expert teachers and those teachers have much to contribute to the conversation about how to train and use others to employ games as learning tools;

2) Games can be relevant for the content you are responsible for teaching and work well as supplemental or integrated media that you share with learners; and

3) Games represent the entertainment arm of a proliferated set of digital tools used across institutions for information and communication - tools that students should be familiar with from an early age - even if playing 'Clifford' games.

4) Games also represent a media that requires learner activation for any progress. They are essentially lean forward media even as entertainment - that have the potential to engage and motivate learners in and around classroom learning topics.

In summary, some games are specifically relevant to a topic and can be used by the teacher for demonstration, some can allow for student adoption of topic matter, some can also be the platform for student creation, and games can also be created to represent ideas and understanding.

Gaining experience with games for learning may mean simply starting with a game and building competency using all approaches with that single game. All four teaching applications can transform games into a powerful addition to classroom learning, but like any skill, they require time, practice, and enduring vision for how they can be used in a practical way. Some games are better for some approaches, naturally, but some provide broader applicability worth investigation.

Interestingly, Minecraft can be used in all four ways.

References

[1] Goldsmith, Marshall. (2013). "Building Happiness, Meaning and Engagement". Games in Education Conference. Malta, NY. Presented Aug. 7, 2013.

[2] Jeanne B Funk, Heidi Bechtoldt Baldacci, Tracie Pasold, Jennifer Baumgardner. "Violence exposure in real-life, video games, television, movies, and the internet: is there desensitization?" Journal of Adolescence, Volume 27, Issue 1, February 2004, Pages 23–39. http://dx.doi.org/10.1016/j. adolescence.2003.10.005.

[3] Bennett, Tom. (2013). Teacher Proof: Why Research in Education Doesn't Always Mean What it Claims, and What you can Do About it. Routledge: New York, NY. Pg. 167.

[4] Gladwell, Malcolm. (2008) Outliers: The Story of Success. Hachette Digital, Inc., 2008. 0316040347, 9780316040341. Online access: http://books.google.com/books/about/Outliers. html?id=3NSImqqnxnkC

[5] Corbett, E. P. J. (1990). Classical rhetoric for the modern student. New York: Oxford University Press., p. 1.; Young, R. E., Becker, A. L., & Pike, K. L. (1970). Rhetoric: discovery and change. New York,: Harcourt Brace & World. p. 1; from Wikipedia http://en.wikipedia.org/wiki/Rhetoric#cite_note-1.

[6] Cuban, L. (1986). *Teachers and machines: The classroom use of technology since 1920.* Teachers College Press.

[7] Cuban, L. (2009). *The blackboard and the bottom line: Why schools can't be businesses.* Harvard University Press.

[8] A special thanks for this distinction goes to: Steinkuehler, C., & Duncan, S. (2008). Scientific habits of mind in virtual worlds. *Journal of Science Education and Technology, 17*(6), 530-543.

[9] Dikkers, S., Martin, J., & Coulter, B. (2012). *Mobile Media Learning: Amazing uses of mobile devices for learning.* Springer-Verlag.

[10] Dewey, J. (2004). *Democracy and education.* Courier Dover Publications.

CHAPTER 2

WHY MINECRAFT?

"The only way kids learn… digital citizenship is by experiencing
social media spaces and being part of those."

- Minecraft Teacher

Looking Closer at Minecraft

In the last chapter we talked about how games can be much more than just titillation. Games can also be vibrant, 'lean forward', media that allows the player far more interactivity than passive media. Games can be tools of creativity and production. In fact, there are scores of games that would warrant a specific guide for using in classrooms, or a study of implementing teachers. So, why Minecraft?

This chapter is an overview of Minecraft. Specifically, before booting up the game or digging into the teacher examples, let's look at what Minecraft is and why Minecraft is worthy of our attention. This chapter attempts to give you a glimpse of the game and explain why this particular game is so compelling for educators.

The game itself is simple. You set up a 'world' filled with randomly generated blocks, and your character is dropped in the middle of the world - empty handed. You can move by using basic keyboard commands (W,A,S,D) and your primary skill is the ability to pick up dirt, wood, or rock (left click) and put it down where you please (right click). While you hold blocks, you can 'craft' them (E) into tools, houses, and armor that allows you to pick up more kinds of blocks. The essential experience is to survive, explore, plan, and build anything you choose - and possibly show your work to a friend.

Minecraft has broken the rules about what we think a video game is, how it should be advertised, and how long a player will invest in their own imagination. It is not enough to say that Minecraft is unique or different and it is insufficient to call it just another computer game. Teachers in this study remember their 'first' time playing Minecraft with fondness. They and millions of others remember the moment they realized they could do *anything* they wanted in a world that was designed for just that.

Minecraft is a special game at the very least. Within the world of gaming, Minecraft is special in four ways:

- The Minecraft experience is about gathering and building whatever you can think of; it is a tool of production at it's core;
- It's also built without a structure or scaffolding that forces certain kinds of experiences. It trusts the player to think;
- Minecraft is social and is appealing because you can play with your friends; and
- The inner guts of Minecraft are wide open to learning more about programming.

Expert players make modifications to the game itself, or 'mods', and the desire to change the game itself is almost as strong as the desire to build, show, and experience the game itself. Any one of these four elements would make Minecraft a great game for educators - probably a top selling game on the market too. But all four of them create something special that is changing an entire generation of play.

It may be overreaching to call it historical, but within reason. "Historical" brings us closer to the context or tone in which players and early adopting teachers have framed it. For those in this study for instance, Minecraft is a not just a game - but a game *changer*.

So, what exactly is so special about this little game? Why would anyone be interested in a game where you move blocks around?

A Blank Slate

Well, for many, 'moving blocks around' needs no explanation. They 'get' it. For others, the idea of the 'blank slate' helps to explain the powerful pull of creation and it's endogenous connection to learning.

Early in American education, students used a small hand held 'slate' and chalk to show their thinking or to work out a problem. A 'blank slate' offered the potential to learn anything, and we still use this phrase to express the idea that anything can be expressed on 'a blank slate' or as a metaphor for students awaiting instruction. Blank slates represent completely open ended potential - as does Minecraft. But Minecraft is better than a blank slate in a few ways too.

Slates, however, were restrictive. They were more expensive than some families could afford at home, they had to be erased each time they were used, and they were small - unless you went to school where they sometimes had giant 'slate boards' on the wall! In this regard, Minecraft is entirely different. The potential of Minecraft is available to everyone relatively cheap, never needs erasing, and can be expansively large.

Today the blank slate has been replaced by paper. Paper allows every student the chance to draw a picture, write a story, take on giant projects, cooperate with others, and share their work. But, paper alone doesn't do anything, it *allows* many things. In teaching and learning, media serves us as a tool to share ideas and for learners to represent ideas back to their educators. While paper can be used for a memo, a picture, a table-top adventure game, a quiz, political commentary, or a sketch of a innovative idea; paper also awaits the users input in all things. This comparison gives us a lens to look at Minecraft too.

Likewise, Minecraft is not a game that you play through. It won't entertain you. Essentially, it won't *do* anything. Minecraft is a randomly generated digital space that you can modify by moving and transforming cube shaped pieces of the world. Playing with other people allows your constructions to be a note to others, a picture or space, a digital adventure game, a test or puzzle, a political agreement, or a chance to build an innovative 3D idea. But before you play, and get a form of writer's block, you should know the nature of this game is that of paper. The user interface is like a pencil, and for non-gamers, you may need to find a player to help if you don't know how to 'hold the pencil' yet. Once you learn, there is no limit to your imagination. Minecraft, like paper, is a blank slate. Minecraft assumes that a blank slate is compelling for many young minds.

Minecraft trusts in a second principle of human nature too. For Minecraft to work, as designed, it assumes that a person's mind is limitless or 'forever, voyaging'.

Forever Voyaging

It seems there was a market for this kind of game too. We know that Minecraft has serious sales. The Wikipedia on Minecraft paints it as one of the top selling games of all time - and it is gaining steam. Before it officially 'released' in 2011, Minecraft beta included 4 million units sold,[1] by 2012 it had grown to 5.3 million copies,[2] and as of this writing in 2013, Minecraft has over 11 million in sales.[3]

<2011	+ 1.0 million copies sold
2011	+ 3.0 million
2012	+ 1.2 million
July 2013	+ 5.8 million
Jan 2013	+ 9.0 million
Total	**20 million copies sold**[4]

Typically computer games, have their top sales the first month they are released and then fade away. Minecraft is selling more copies this year than two years ago and has sold more copies each year than the year previous. Heck, in the last 24 hours alone, they have sold over fifteen thousand copies,[5] - enough to launch a small indie company.

Minecraft, without a publisher, and without one paid advertisement spread via *word of mouth*[6] to be a central hobby for millions. This is much less like a typical entertainment product, that is consumed and forgotten, and much more like what we would expect to see when a new innovative technology releases. The first exposure to the game is the same.

Minecraft is not outwardly impressive. The typical first impression of Minecraft is to be a bit disappointed, 'So *this* is what all the hype is about?!?' Minecraft does not strike awe into the first time player. Though it requires a good graphics card to render, you'll notice first that it's graphics appear to be a throwback to the mid-90's. It looks like a 'retro' game.

We've already pointed out that there isn't much more than a blank slate to look at. The game is full of cubes, no motion capture has been done for your characters movement, and you don't need a retina display to see the chunky graphics. The soundtrack does its best to lull you to sleep and the standard 'getting started' tutorial is conspicuously missing. Minecraft seemingly breaks all the rules of awesome game design' because it fails to provide clear direction, narrative, or context; it doesn't scale (much) through more and more challenging 'levels'; and there is no central or essential challenge for you to overcome.

Not only is Minecraft *not* visually impressive, there is a steep imagination curve that pushes away casual players. If you don't have an avid fan, (bearing the fruits of creative thoughts), showing you the game, you too may start it up and think, 'Really? This is all there is?' Or worse, you'll fall in a dark square hole, get stuck, and decide to move on to other games in complete frustration.

Current players have tried to make it easy for you though. If you go online, you'll find an assortment of Minecraft Startup guides to help new players navigate the first day and night of the game. Chapter 3 will help with this also, but my goal is not to get you playing, but to have you forever voyaging to new classroom ideas.

It isn't the production that makes Minecraft draw millions, it's that millions can produce within Minecraft - and do. Like paper, Minecraft requires the player's action for anything to happen. It's a lean forward media. Minecraft simply opens up a world in which you choose the adventure, you choose the goals, you choose who to play with, and you build whatever you want. It assumes and trusts that the player has a mind that wants to create, that can make it's own plans, and will connect and help others learn to play. Like a blank slate, the power isn't in the slate, it's in the potential of the media. In Minecraft, the designers trust that the player has a mind, and, in the words of William Wordsworth (via Steve Meretsky), that the mind is forever voyaging.

> Of Newton with his prism and silent face,
>
> The marble index of a mind for ever
>
> Voyaging through strange seas of Thought, alone.[7]

It takes a unique restraint for a designer to hand over the reins of design to the consumer - or a trust and respect even. One has to believe in humanity a bit. In this regard, educators can resonate a bit with blank slates, paper, Lego's... and Minecraft.

Minecraft humbly presents a randomly generated world when you set it up. Players are faced with a silent 'index' of options that they can alight with a sharp mind. Thinking is an internally rewarding experience and creator, Markus "Notch" Persson, is to be credited with making a game that trusts and relies on player thought to fill the space with intention.

This explains why Minecraft was, and probably had to be, a non-corporate decision to make. Notch started his own company, Mojang, to make this game where the 'Sea of Thought' can also be lonely, filled with 'creeping' terrors, frustrating, yet ultimately rewarding. This requires a trust in the intelligence of the player to fill their own worlds.

Or perhaps this trust wasn't such a leap of faith? Mojang also built a new kind of multi-player mode that encouraged real life friendships to make private worlds together. Where one person may come up short, playing with others is a far more generative activity. Humans are, after all, social beings. If one person couldn't muster the voyaging mind, perhaps two or more people together could cultivate the needed creativity and play to populate this game?

Embracing a Limited Multiplayer Online Game

For years, I thought I knew what online play was all about, but when my kids dug into Minecraft, their experience had some key differences - namely Minecraft was a limited multiplayer online (LMO) game.

The Story of a Gamer...

I'd been actively involved in a 'guild' of online gamers. We had large group events, 'raids', on Saturday nights and Sunday afternoons, but fellow guildies were generally online every night - so if you were looking for a small pick-up group, you could usually find one. We played online in Massive Multiplayer Online Role Playing Games, or MMORPGs, or for short, MMOs. We were a 'family friendly' guild and considered ourselves less intense than 'hardcore' gamers. We played for fun.

My role was that of 'tank' and I loved drawing the attention of big, nasty creatures and taunting them to hit me. While I was tossed about, my friends would pummel the 'boss' of baddies and heal me until we conquered the latest challenge game makers threw at us. These weekly efforts usually resulted in conquest, but at times it took us a month to topple one of these boss fights.

Our core group had played for nine years - jumping from Everquest to World of Warcraft together the week that WoW was released. This was my gathering place each weekend or what Constance Steinkuehler calls my digital 'third space' between work and family life.[8] Using annual vacations, my digital friends had gradually become face to face friends too. We enjoyed each others time. We shared a common interest, were willing to share the same amount of time, and generally enjoyed sharing life with each other each week. Over these years, we also got pretty good at tackling the challenges of MMOs together. We were coming to be known as one of the best guilds on one of the most competitive servers in the game.

However, as our guild was successfully beating baddies, this came with challenges. As people came, they needed leadership, communication, and management to organize 50-60 active players (150-200 players were occasional members). Also, when people gather, so does drama. We had to handle drama and would inevitably had to meet and agree on guild rules, policy, and direction.

In fact, while real life had me working as a high school principal, I was always learning tips for my real job from how we led our guild online. People management skills crossed the digital line just fine for me. After all people are people. (I should point to what I believe to be seminal work by Moses Wolfenstein[9] who tracked this phenomena of transferred leadership skills across school leaders playing MMOs.)

This alone was interesting for a time. But eventually, I would hesitate before logging in and consider if I wanted to take on whatever was waiting. After all, work is work. Some nights, after working with people all day, I just didn't have the will to log in.

Even when the game became tedious, I still jumped online once a week to maintain very real relationships with people. But they could tell I was less committed to the guild, raiding, and managing people. For a full year, I dutifully took damage for them as a tank, worked on the latest armor upgrades, and trained my kids to run 'dailies' for me to offset time on redundant collection quests - but I also stepped back from the social engagements. Yet I still logged in to announce to my friends that I was going to 'log out' for good.

Still, a few close friends and I are regularly in touch and game together occasionally. So that was a long story that led to this reality for me. My core group of digital friends and I are still in touch. It was that small group of players that made the time social for me, not the scores of people crowding the server, but the few relationally relevant people that could laugh, play, and share time that was rewarding.

The truth was, I enjoyed their company, but just couldn't justify playing a MMO that was starting to feel like a job. This is where Minecraft is a welcomed change of pace in the gaming world. It hit the market at a perfect time after a wave of MMOs hit the market and before people had abandoned them entirely.

For both veteran guildies, like myself, and for millions of new players, like my kids, Minecraft came with many of the design benefits of an MMO, but the low-key playful nature of what I'll call an *Limited* Multiplayer Online experience - or LMO. You can play with friends. You can set up times to meet online or see what the other has done while you logged out. You can plan together, show off 'awesome' projects, or set up challenges for others to enjoy. Playing together is fun and a key aspect of gaming expectations today.

Teacher concerns

Yet, during my time working with teachers across the country, I see a pattern of hesitation toward MMOs in the classroom. Teachers are justifiably shy of MMOs because they have no control over who is going to talk to their students once online. A typical MMO server could have between two and ten thousand players online at any time - which presents the *potential* of the wrong people chatting with students.

As exciting, social, and investing as these games are, teachers have to sell new curricular ideas to parents and administrators. So if there are thousands online, how can you prevent bullies? How do you stop a stranger from asking for my child's address? What if they see a swear word? For gamers, these are minimal problems (if not imaginary), however, for administration seeking to avoid a lawsuit, these are central possibilities. It's the potential problem that can freeze educational innovations sometimes, not the actual issues.

MMOs provide no guarantee of privacy because they are designed to be social experiences. (In their defense, you can report inappropriate play and the MMO companies are pretty diligent in following up on these complaints). Developers want you to be able to meet new people, and do everything they can to facilitate social play and positive online norms of behavior. Players can and do get banned, but game companies wait for abuses to happen first, then react.

Educators attempt to prevent abuses before they happen. Socially, MMOs are more like going to a concert, and less like having a 'sleepover' with a few friends and parent supervision. Why not invite over kids you can trust, whose parents you can report to, and keep them in your own home which you can guarantee is safe? There may be bouncers, hired for safety, at a concert that respond to bad behavior, but as a parent or teacher, why bother until the kids are older?

For my part, I completely agree with this bias. Schools should and are well served in protecting kids from as many dangers and hazards as they can. It is the teacher's job to make the case that they can combine great learning experiences within a safe context for the kids. LMOs offer this kind of guaranteed protection and are a much easier game to present to kids for this reason alone. So far, Minecraft is the first to really nail this controlled multiplayer option in it's native game.

So, while my work in the past[10] has been to study teachers that have overcome these resistant points for great classroom learning, it hasn't gone viral in schools. These challenges have made the use of MMOs in classroom settings fairly limited. The LMO however, addresses many of these concerns.

LMOs for Learning

Most people have had private (controlled participation) social gatherings and have attended (open uncontrolled participation) large community events. Both social experiences are integrated into our lives and are far from exclusive of each other. So it's not hard to imagine that games would eventually be designed to address both styles of social connections.

In fact, there have been other 'invite only' multiplayer games. Some of the very first local area network games were by invite only, strategy games have long allowed you to invite a friend to play chess, scrabble, or Civilization. These games require a degree of coordination or act as 'play by mail' asynchronous communication. Players exchange 'moves' but little informal communication or 'hanging out' together.

However, the excitement of having an environment that is 'live' is a different sort of social connection. Setting up a server creates an 'always on' setting. This means that anyone can login and play as they please and that when you login, you are likely to find friends there to chat with or take on a new adventure together. So what MMOs offer is community and conversation in a way that other multiplayers do not. An LMO, may have less players, however, the players it does have are all people that you have chosen to have in your community.

This is a significant advance for teachers. Minecraft offers all the stimulation, cognition, and social interactivity of an MMO, but without the worries that playing with strangers will lead to. A teacher can set up a class, make a whitelist of players, and say with complete certainty that the space is safe for school use. In fact, for the paranoid, they can set up *internal* servers at the school or a *local network* in the computer lab that has no connection to the internet itself at all.

This kind of LMO retains the benefits, and eliminates the worries of community style online games.

Modding

Minecraft is a blank slate; it allows for a voyaging mind; it is an LMO; and Minecraft represents a fourth trend in digital gaming that has engaged a new generation of media producers - modding. A 'Mod' is short for a modification to a piece of software, especially a game. Modding is the verbing of the word and is the act of making mods - an activity apart from the game itself, but is seen as an act of expert fandom around the game.

Most mods are not kept secret, they are published online for anyone to download and attach to their own game. Mods can change the graphics, rules, or any other aspect of the game itself. Increasingly, game companies encourage and welcome these modifications because they actually can serve to improve or fix issues in the game released. Modding communities also build momentum for a game and a self-organized community around the game. Under the radar, game companies can also scan the modders for experts that may be worth hiring.

For instance top shelf games are embracing modding for their games. The popular Skyrim uses the Steam Workshop space for players to make their own stories, objects in the game, or add spells, and change rules. Players usually find a thing or two in the games user interface (UI) that bugs them, so they go into the code, change it, and share their fix with the world. Mods thus allow players to customize their play experience in every regard. Expert World of Warcraft player screens are often filled with such UI mods and in some ways raiding depends on the modding community to build tools for leaders. Even my lifetime favorite Civilization has opened up to modders that convert the game, add world leaders, change units, and allow for core rule changes to play. Mods customize, add play-time, and field prototypes for future game designs based on player desires.

Expert modders become famous for their work - within that gaming community at least. But when a game has 7-15 million players and 1-2 hundred thousand have downloaded your mod, that is more famous than most politicians, scholars, or even many entertainers. Of course it's a different kind of fame, for a different type of media, but it's still fame. Top modders will have followers that know they do good work, bug test, and generally have similar taste. And for many novice gamers, the aspiration to make a mod and be known for it is a powerful draw.

So in one sense Minecraft simply follows this trend. It too opens up the files for players to change and modify. In another sense, Minecraft takes modding a step further. Minecraft hosts one of the largest, and growing, community of players so the stability of interest means your mod will be relevant to a larger number of players and for a longer time than most games. But that isn't all, Minecraft opens up the doors to modding like no other game.

Because Minecraft is on simple to set up servers, with fairly basic graphics, and contains little to no storyline, it allows players access to nearly every aspect of game play. Setting up a server allows you to change the game world to your taste and gives the player a chance to see that changing code can make the game more fun for you. When players start to add friends, they inevitably have to negotiate the 'rules' of the world server so they can compromise on a mutually fun space.

Sooner or later, one of the players finds out that they can upload new 'skins' for their characters, which are seen by all. Instead of endless farming to get the cool gear though, in

Minecraft you can simply modify your graphics files. Using editors you can design your own skins and make your characters look like a superhero, a robot, a princess, or anything you can imagine.

Once a player has tinkered with server setup and graphics mods, the idea that you can go into the game and add unique operations and objects is suddenly much more approachable. So the progression and natural scaffolding for programming feels easier. Though there is no clear data, I'd presume that far fewer Tomb Raider players mod the game than do Minecraft players, simply because Tomb Raider can be a completely rewarding experience without mods and even without other players. Minecraft is already a tool for creation, attracts creative people, and makes modding an integrated and rewarding part of the experience.

On a side note, some are arguing that everyone should learn to code.[11] That every subject, every institution, and every profession will be led by those that can master and *produce* in the media that transmits communication and information. Today, they argue computers are the media of choice for doing work across professions. This leads to a question of how and where to introduce coding to youth? So as these folks are building online guides and tutorials, Minecraft quietly has millions of youth learning to set up servers, build graphics, and modify code to suit their play styles.

In Chapter 9, we'll introduce you to all of these forms of modding in the game and show you a few tricks. For now, understand that modding is part of the context of this game and part of why this game is uniquely worth taking a look at for classroom use.

Not only is Minecraft full of potential, designed for thinking, and social, it's an entry level drug for programming and creating digital realities. These four aspects of Minecraft make it interesting within gaming culture as a truly unique and innovative piece of software, but these elements also have easy to see educational benefits before you even boot up the game.

This is true outside of any curriculum you design, or any topic you want to cover. Like slates, paper and legos, the tools of creation are open to any activity you choose to attach them too. This particular tool has the additional benefit of being wired for social engagement and programming skills. This follows an age old educational principle of modeling learning. If you want learners to write, hook them on reading and show them they can write too. If you want engineers, hook them on legos and show them mini motors. If you want students to learn today's digital tools, you can use digital tools for learning; one way is hooking them on Minecraft and showing them what they can do with mods.

That is why this book is focused on one game.

So, Why Minecraft?

Because it's a digital tool that provides learners a blank slate, moddable, LMO to forever voyage the imagination. Just ask students that play and you will get some convincing material, as one of the teachers I interviewed found:

> "So there have been 70 middle school girls running their own world and it blows my mind what must go on in this server so he had each of them type up a paragraph for his own reasons about what Minecraft has taught me. I took that stack of letters and I gave them to my principal and I think that was the final push she needed to give this a try."

Together, these assets have made it much easier to find teachers integrating Minecraft into their classrooms. In fact, unlike most research efforts, the Minecraft teachers largely *came to me* when they heard I was doing this book. Minecraft has an emergent, active, and passionate community of educators already using it for learning - and they care about sharing this tool with you! Teachers are like that. When they see a good thing, they are ready to share it because they see the larger mission of serving the kids.

Actually, I'm humbled a bit by the task of doing justice to what they are so excited about. This book isn't so much my thinking about Minecraft (or MC), but my effort to adequately represent what the teachers in the study want to tell you. They wanted to make sure you knew the ease of use, that you weren't scared off by the learning curve, and that you had examples of use that you could relate to. That is what this book is hoping to accomplish.

So it's time to boot up. Minecraft is easy to use and the next chapter should have you move from reading this book to playing the game to see what it's all about for yourself. After you've played for a bit, you are ready to return to Chapter 4 and find out what teachers have done to make this part of their classrooms.

References

[1] "Minecraft beta cracks 4 million". *GameSpot*. CBS Interactive. Retrieved November 9, 2011.

[2] Shields, Duncan (March 22, 2012). "Top 15 best selling PC games of all time". SK Gaming. Retrieved January 16, 2013.

[3] "Minecraft stats". https://minecraft.net/stats. Retrieved July 30, 2013.

[4] Nunneley, Stephany (January 22, 2013). "Minecraft sales hit 20 million mark for all platforms". *VG247*. Retrieved January 30, 2013.

[5] "Minecraft stats" https://minecraft.net/stats. Retreived Aug 21, 2013.

[6] Silverman, Matt (October 1, 2010). "Minecraft: How Social Media Spawned a Gaming Sensation". *Mashable*. Mashable Inc. Retrieved December 28, 2012.

[7] Wordsworth, W. *The Prelude: Book First*. use by Stephen Meretsky's Text Adventure Game *A Mind Forever Voyaging*. http://www.bartleby.com/145/ww287.html. Retrieved August 27, 2013.

[8] Steinkuehler, C. and D. Williams (2006). "Where everybody knows your (screen) name: Online games as "third places"." Journal of Computer-Mediated Communication 11(4).

[9] As a side note, I was part of a unique study by Moses Wolfenstein on the links between online guild gaming and real life leadership practices. Look up his dissertation for more.

[10] Dikkers, S. (2012). The Professional Development Trajectories of Teachers Successfully Integrating and Practicing with New Information and Communication Technologies. Curriculum and Instruction. Madison, WI, University of Wisconsin - Madison. PhD.

[11] See intro video at http://www.code.org/.

Further Reading:

Review http://www.bbc.co.uk/news/magazine-23572742

HOW DO I START PLAYING?

Mike Cisneros and Seann Dikkers

"I played it for 12 months before I was even thinking of bringing it into the classroom."

"So, I think the best advice I can give is to just jump into it."

- Minecraft Teacher

A First Time for Everything

Last week, I was at a conference and was asked to do a 'workshop' session with teachers and show them *Minecraft*. When we arrived… the assigned room had no computers in it. With great flexibility the teachers were willing to review 'Plan B' slides of the game and talk about the teachers that we highlight in this book. We spent the next hour in a delightful conversation about how important it was to test out software for yourself. Normally a video game workshop without computers would be a problem, but it wasn't. The teachers went home, played, and wrote back to share that their play time experiences were outstanding!

Many of these teachers knew a young player that could coach them through it. They stayed after school for a day and had one or more walk them along and encourage them each time they got stuck. In fact, as we interviewed MC teachers, they often recommended this pathway to learning MC. If you know a younger player, have them show you. If you do not, I thought it would be a treat to present this chapter as close to this form as possible. Mike Cisneros is an avid MC player and was willing to let me use our conversations below and is thus a co-author on this chapter. As you read, notice how teaching and learning in this context is a natural, encouraging, process. Mike is a clear and natural teacher - driven by his love of the game.

The following, then, is a simple step by step prompting on how to play *Minecraft*. For new gamers, we'll walk you through it. For veteran gamers, this may still be interesting as a case of informal digital instruction. For new players, I would still encourage you to read only if you run into troubles - it's good to go run into some troubles first. The game comes with minimal instruction and encourages you to look around, set your own goals, and grab a friend or student when you get stuck. For some, this vagueness is part of the fun.

Two quick reminders: First, don't confuse your ability to navigate a game with its capacity to be a powerful tool in the classroom. Think of when you first picked up a pencil, or when you first used a camera - it may have felt awkward. Expect a learning curve. Second, remember you don't really *have* to get good at navigating digital worlds before you manage a classroom of players. Students can demo, help with navigation, and joyfully watch you learn.

Playing *Minecraft* is part of your lesson preparation in using it. Later in the book, when we look at teachers who use *Minecraft*, there will be many references to the game itself that will make much more sense if you've played it yourself. Also, most of the teachers in this study (15 of 17) played the game before deciding to use it in classes; the other two had a fellow teacher that they were working with who had played it. So go play. Put down this book, navigate to https://minecraft.net/download and follow the instructions. Plan on giving it an evening or at least an hour or two before coming back.

Learning to Play Minecraft

Seann Dikkers: Hey Mike, thanks for this conversation. Before we dig in, tell me what you like about playing MC.

Mike Cisneros: The thing I enjoy the most about Minecraft is that it's versatile. Literally any person, in any mindset, can play it. If you just want to build with your friends, you are able to create a server and play with them! Another thing, Minecraft is that it is very straightforward; to get wood you cut down a tree, to get sand you find a beach, if you want some steak or leather you hunt down some cows.

---

1) Setting up your account

SD: Moo! Alright, so treat me like I'm a brand new player - a newbie. What do I do first?

MC: First you have to make an account on Minecraft.net. Once there, go to the top right corner and click [Register].

- Fill in the personal information,
- Click the green [Register] button at the bottom, and
- Confirm your email address.

Later, you can choose to try the demo or buy the game. Just use those prompts.

SD: Do I need to worry about getting spam from Minecraft/Mojang? Can my students use a fake email instead of their school email accounts?

MC: Yes, there are options such as *"I would like to receive e-letters from Minecraft/Mojang."* If you don't want these updates, make sure you don't select this option while signing up for an account. Sign up using an email account you can access regularly, whether that be an email address you already have, one you set up just for Minecraft, or even your school email address.

---

2) Downloading *Minecraft*

SD: Ok, so I'm registered. Now what?

MC: Now you need to download it on your computer. This may be different depending on what operating system you are using. First:

- Go to Minecraft.net
- Sign in (if you aren't already)
- Click the [Download Now!] button...

For Apple operating systems:

- Right below [Minecraft for Mac OS X] there will be a file named "Minecraft.dmg",
- Click "Minecraft.dmg" to download it to your computer,
- After the file is downloaded, double click on it to open it,
- Confirm that you understand you downloaded this [may appear based on your settings],
- Drag the Minecraft Application into your 'Applications' folder as instructed. (This will make place an icon in the folder and on your 'launchpad'. You can drag it to your 'dock' if you want easy access later),
- Open the Minecraft Application by double clicking on it,
- Log into Minecraft when prompted (Use the registration we just set up), and
- Click the "Play!" button at the bottom of the page.

For Windows operating systems:

- Right below "Minecraft for Windows" there will be a file named "Minecraft.exe",
- Click "Minecraft.exe" to download it to your computer,
- After the file is downloaded, open it,
- Once it is open, click "Run",

- Log into Minecraft when prompted to, and
- Click the "Play!" button at the bottom of the page

---

3) Generating a World

SD: So far so good. I'm going to press on [Singleplayer] for now...

Image 1: Minecraft Startup Screen

MC: Right, later on, you may want to look at the options you have for the game on the startup screen, but for now lets get you playing by pressing [Create New World] next.

SD: Done. I'm naming my world now...

MC: While you do that there is a single middle button that toggles what kind of world you want. When you click on it it will rotate between three settings: [Game Mode Survival], [Game Mode Hardcore], and [Game Mode Creative]. For now, lets play what the community calls 'Vanilla Minecraft' and stay on Survival.

[More World Options...] allows you to customize your world a bit. This is where you can pick a 'seed', or pre-made world, but we won't do that to start. [Structures] are signs of life in your world. [World Type] are options that tell the generator what kind of geography you want. It will still be random, but you can go with lots of hills, or flat as a board.

SD: Why would that matter?

MC: Because when you start playing a bit, it changes the challenge and setting for what you build and how you adventure in the game. Some players just like to explore the world, for instance, so they do [World Type: Amplified] to get impossible mountains and otherworldly landscapes. [World Type: Flat] is more for builders that don't want to do as much terraforming for their designs.

Leave [Allow Cheats: ON], we'll use those to get you started. Also leave [Bonus Chest: OFF] it's cheating.

SD: [laughs!] So it's cheating to have a chest, and not cheating to have cheats?

MC: Yes, that's about it. [laughs]. You have a point there. Cheats are different in a game like this. It's not cheating to get shortcuts to managing the game itself, it is cheating to skip over newbie content that really helps you learn. Cheating to save time is good, cheating to skip learning is bad.

SD: That's fascinating Mike, really it is. We need to spend more time on that idea later.

MC: For now, click [Done], and you return to 'Create New World'. Click on [Create New World] and it will start generating one for you.

---

4) Moving around and Monsters!!

SD: It is running! I used "W.A.S.D" keys to move around, looks like the space bar lets me jump... and now there is a green thing chasing me!

MC: That green thing is a Creeper, eventually they blow up if you get too close, so just keep running, or stop and let it blow up. Arrow keys work for moving too. You can use your mouse to 'look around' too, most experienced players get good at using the [W] and the mouse together to move around. New players have trouble with that.

SD: AAAAAAH! He exploded on me! I don't like those!

MC: [Laughs at my misfortune!] Lets turn them off. Return to the game menu by pressing [ESC] on your keyboard. Choose [Options...] and in the top right click on [Difficulty] until you see [Difficulty:Peaceful], then [Done] and [Back to Game].

For new players the monsters create a need in the game. You need to build shelter! The first thing you should do is to gather supplies and build some type of protection against monsters. Monsters, or "mobs," spawn in the dark, so consider building a house before the sun goes down! In the morning the light burns them up so you get some time to explore and collect.

---

5) Collecting Supplies

MC: Typically, when starting off in Minecraft, you will use anything from your surroundings to make a shelter. When you first spawn, you will be in something called a "biome." There are 12 main biomes, most have wood. Wood is probably the most useful resource in the game, you can make tools, weapons, and even build a house out of it!

SD: Sure, there are trees over there… birch! I'm running to them now.

MC: To collect a block of wood, approach the tree and use your mouse to move the plus sign (+) in the middle of your screen on top of the block you want to harvest. You hold down the left mouse button to break it, (keep holding down the mouse button, it takes a few seconds), and then walk over the block to collect it. You can collect all the wood you want!

Image 2 & 3: (L) Harvesting Wood, (R) Harvested Wood

---

6) Crafting

MC: Crafting is a huge part of the game (hence the name MineCRAFT). To access your crafting table and inventory simply press [E].

SD: Okay, I see lots of blocks.

MC: Yes, here you can craft the 'block' of wood into wood planks. Drag (left click and hold) the wood blocks into the crafting table and it will show that you can craft wood planks.

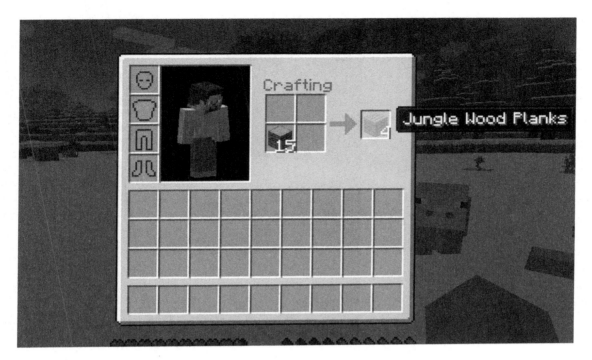

Image 4: Crafting Wood into Planks

To collect the wood planks, either drag the planks into your inventory (or press [Shift]+[Right Click] to turn all of your wood blocks into planks at once. Now you are crafting blocks that have greater uses within the game, than just the raw material you first mined.

---

7) Building a House

MC: Once you have materials, you can start making a house. Begin trying to find a flat part on the ground. I found this area in a nearby tundra biome and it will work perfectly for my new house. Harvest enough wood to build a modest shelter for yourself. Mine was 7x7 blocks with a space for a door.

So now you're ready to start building. With your inventory [E] open, drag and drop your building materials into the 'toolbar' at the bottom of your inventory. Click [E] again to return to the game interface. See how the toolbar is still 'in game' too?

Image 5: A Starter House

SD: Yes, so I can use anything on that bar while playing?

MC: Yes, if your planks are ready, to place a block, first use the mouse scroll wheel (or number keys) to select the planks, then target [+] any existing block surface and [Right Click] to place the planks. You can place a block from any direction on any side of an existing block. Keep stacking blocks and you should be able to build a shelter. Use the [space bar] to jump on top of a block and stack higher. Use [left click] to remove one you don't want. A few more crafting tips to finish your house.

---

8) Finishing off a house

MC: You probably need a door now.

SD: Yes, and a roof… but it looks like I can add blocks from below too. Up to three blocks away from my character. So, how do I make a door?

MC: So for that you need to craft a larger crafting table. The one [E] we've been using only has four spaces to put materials, we need more. So to make a crafting table, fill all for spaces with a wood plank, you can split 'piles' of wood by [right clicking] on them in the crafting window. Now you'll see a 'Crafting Table' ready to drag to your toolbar?

SD: Sure.

MC: Drag it onto your toolbar and leave the crafting window. Highlight the new crafting table on your toolbar [scroll wheel/number keys] and place [right click] the crafting table inside your house on the ground. [Right click] on the crafting table and it will open a crafting screen, like yours [E] but with more space now. Now you can make a door with those wooden planks.

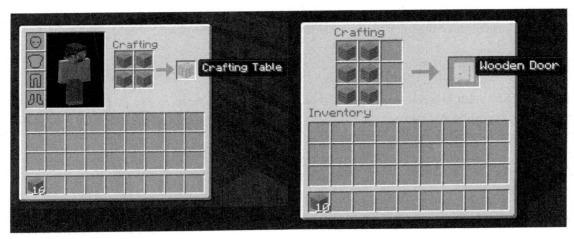

Image 6 & 7: (L) Making a Crafting Table, (R) Making a Wooden Door

While you're in your crafting table, you want to fill the left and middle columns with wood planks. Move the door to your hotbar, leave the crafting window, highlight the door, then place [right click] the door in the doorway of your house.

SD: Home, sweet home. I feel like a pioneer or an island castaway making my way in the wilderness.

MC: [laughs] Yes, so do a few million other people!

---

9) Forever Mornings

MC: Did you shut off monsters?

SD: I think I left them on.

MC: If you die in the game, you will be teleported back to where you first spawned when you first started the game. So no worries. If you built your house near the original point, you should be able to just run back to it. Making a bed and sleeping in it will make the night go, but that is later in the game. For now, lets save you time and keep having fun building.

SD: How do I do that?

MC: We 'cheat' the natural day and night cycle. Because you left the 'cheats' on when you set up the world, the designers gave you a lot of control over the world. Some gamers want the game to be hard and the 'learning curve' is better when it's more challenging. So the monsters are your foil to building, hunting, farming, and generally doing what you want. But I find that most adults just don't get that this challenge (part of the fun for me) is exactly why it's fun to succeed. Without challenge, your victories are minimal.

SD: I think for an adult the challenge is just getting around and figuring out the buttons.

MC: Well, the next first person game you play, you'll see the buttons are all the same. These are pretty common conventions for gamers. So for kids, it's the monsters that frustrate and validate achievements.

SD: That makes sense and makes it easier for me to want to 'cheat' for now. How do I make it morning.

MC: The designers give you all the tools, so it's 'gamer-cheating'. Press [T], for [T]alk, on your keyboard. This brings up a bar you can type in at the bottom left of the screen. Type, [/time set 0]. That makes it dawn and you have a full day ahead of you again.

SD: Nice, forever morning!

---

10) Monsters

SD: So what if I wanted to leave the monsters on?

MC: I was hoping you'd ask. If you leave monsters on (ESC>Options...>Difficulty), you'll need to defend yourself or hide. Just run from the green 'Creepers', they explode and aren't worth doodling with at this point in the game. If you get up close, you'll hear a "SSSST" sound that sets the explosion. They stop moving when this starts, so you can run away in time.

To defend yourself use that crafting table to make a sword and keep it handy on your toolbar. You can make one out of wood pretty easily.

MC: Use two sticks for a handle and you can start making all sorts of tools like a Shovel (for digging), a Pick Axe (for mining), a hoe (for farming), and an axe (for speeding up how long it takes you to harvest wood. Play around with this and make a few tools. Using stone instead of wood will upgrade the tools to make them faster and last longer. You'll need a pick axe to harvest stone. To find it, just dig a few layers of dirt and you'll find it - or explore for a hillside with exposed rock.

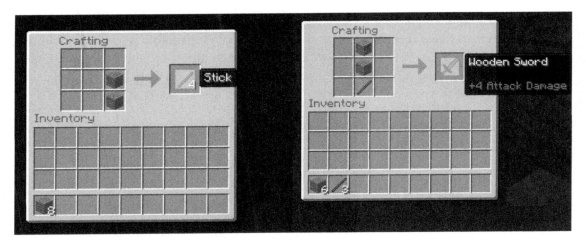

Image 8 & 9: (L) Making a Stick, (R) Making a Sword

SD: Can I use tools to fight monsters.

MC: Sure, but the sword hits harder. You have other options besides fighting too.

SD: Like?

MC: That house you built is your first and finest defence, to play survival MC, just hide out and play with your craft table a bit during the evenings. You can also build more elaborate defences to ward them off - moats, walls, traps.

Light also repels them from 'spawning' (automatic monster generation) nearby too. You'll want to learn how to make a torch and place them all around your house.

SD: How do I make a torch?

MC: A stick and coal - or charcoal. But I think this is the point to show you a resource that nearly all MC players find out about...

---

11) Building Everything

SD: What's that?

MC: Here is the link: http://minecraft.gamepedia.com/Crafting#Complete_recipe_list

Anything in the game can be searched and they show you a neat little picture of how to arrange materials in your crafting table. Torches are in there.

Early on, you'll want to make a Chest, Furnace, better tools (with stone and iron), and eventually learn to make food. To eat food you put it on your toolbar and hold down the mouse button. You'll see your hand come up and 'munch' the food until it's gone. That's later though. You have all you need at this point to keep going and learn as you need using Minecraft wiki's like the one above.

SD: Thanks Mike, you are amazing! So what do I do now? What's the point of the game?

MC: [laughs] The point is to play. Use your imagination, explore, build, adventure, dig, or anything. You can do anything. It's like legos. If you have to ask what to do, you've forgotten what being a kid is all about. You've also forgotten how to invent your own purpose, and maybe it's high time you start working on that.

Mike Cisneros is a student at Ohio University from Cincinnati, Ohio. He is currently studying at the School of Media Arts & Studies with his focus in video production and video game design.

CHAPTER 4

WHY STUDY TEACHERS?

"Its worlds that are opened up that are different than
the ones students live in today."

- Minecraft teacher

Metaphors for Teacher Learners

In most fields of practice, there is a robust and interested audience for understanding how the top practitioners perceive and conduct their work. For instance, in business, we see shelves filled with biographies and memoirs from top CEO's; in medicine, leading doctors publish new methods and potential cures to the rest of the community; in politics, new campaigning tactics are debriefed by insiders and arm chair commentators for months following an election. But what of educators? How do we approach teacher learning?

Teachers as Employees

If teachers are employees, shouldn't we be able to tell them to use digital technology in the classroom and they obey? Reform should be easy to initiate, but it is not. Many ask why this is the case, and logically pursue 'primers' on more effective professional development (Desimone, 2011) strategies. These are based on researched 'best practices' found in successful districts. Others document and define successful learning phenomena, like communities of practice (Cox, 2005), and seek to expand them through mandated participation. These approaches are 'top down' in essence. They propose that teachers serve districts, and districts have historically guided teacher practice. So, when we present new ideas, teachers should embrace them because it is their job.

This assumes that with the right inputs, teachers will react consistently to the 'best' ideas. When they do not, this research logically starts to identify 'barriers'[1] to teacher adoption

---

[1] Rogers, P. L. (2000). Barriers to adopting emerging technologies in education. *Journal of Educational Computing Research, 22*(4), 455-472.

like fidelity, 'resistance', toxic cultures, lack of resources, laziness, or other wrenches in the machine - all are well documented[2] by those that research *employees*. This approach places a premium on convincing or compelling new practices and has often led to concerted efforts to unify teacher evaluation, curriculum, and standardized tests to place pressure on teachers to 'change' for the better. However, when it comes to teaching digital literacies, integrating reading or math across the curriculum, or data-driven decision making, low adoption rates seem to confound centralized planning. Teacher 'employees' can list a variety of reasons why technology is not getting used (barriers) and they prove very resilient to new ideas.

Say you want to change classroom practices. If the teacher is an *employee*, you should not have to study what they do at home, informal learning, or influences. Why would you? As an employee, they should comply with what you tell them to do! The problem, then, is in clearly telling them what to do - via in-service training. It makes more sense that you study and perfect PD deliveries that provide the best results or gets the most teachers 'on board' with your program. This has been the path of many reform efforts that have come and gone the last few decades - but these efforts have ultimately not shown large scale adoption. Despite the overwhelming focus on employees, teachers remain an elusive bunch.

Teachers as Conservants

What if teachers were better understood as independent actors that have agency in order to protect the teaching and learning process? What if schools are supposed to be tough to change? Other scholars point out the inherent *conservative* nature of educational practice (Postman, 1979). They point out that the entire education system, in the United States, was intentionally designed as a 'loosely coupled system' (Elmore, 2000) that serves to insulate classrooms from the whims and fads of changing workplaces and politics. Education is too important to allow teachers to be overly pressured by powerful outside lobbies, so teachers are the *conservators* of a great institution - and rightly so. Despite pop culture excitement for innovation or proponents of new technology, when a teacher closes their classroom door, they can essentially do what they feel is effective and have a moral obligation to innovate or conserve as appropriate. This allows top practitioners to practice for decades and quietly deliver innovative and outstanding lessons despite tidal reform efforts washing by.

This understanding of teacher practice does allow for much more patience over time, and can adequately explain slower or stalled adoption of new ideas in education. For a new idea to take root, it has to be shown worthy of adoption, over a *generation* of teachers, and leaders need to consider how to convince, not dictate. If not, districts can buy costly new technology, that largely goes unused in practice (Cuban, 2009), and not be able to force

---

[2] Wachira, P., & Keengwe, J. (2011). Technology integration barriers: Urban school mathematics teachers perspectives. *Journal of Science Education and Technology, 20*(1), 17-25.

teachers to use it. The conserving view of teachers provides for understanding why teachers may choose not to adopt new practice, but provides less direction for understanding why some do. It is worth noting, still, that teachers have authority over their day-to-day practice, and that this provides a precious protection for education to not be dominated by industry, politics, or fads.

If teachers are primarily *conservators*, then it makes sense for change agents to investigate essentially different system designs that allow teachers far less control over classrooms. So, automated online settings, removal of tenure protections, common core curriculums, and/ or a more centralized systems of accountability and pressure for teachers should result in transformed learning systems that produce better change - but they do not. In fact, it is increasingly obvious that increasing pressure on schools is not having measurable impact on student learning.

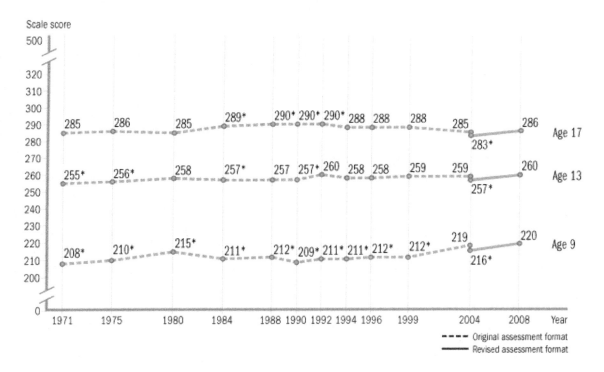

Image 1: Trend in NAEP reading average scores for 9-, 13-, and 17-year-old students

This is a hot button issue, I know, and you may resonate with one of these two approaches to influencing schools. My point is that to direct teachers or to undermine their independence may not have a measurable impact on either teachers adoption of new practices or on student learning overall.

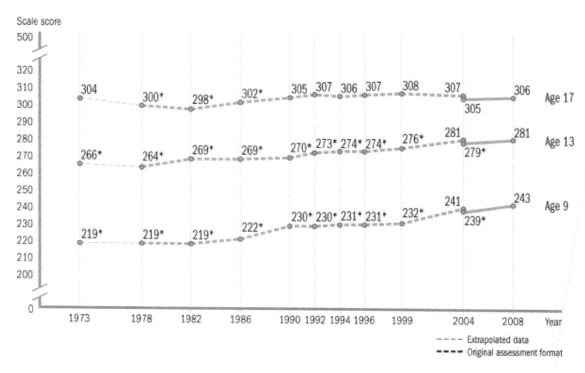

Image 2: Trend in NAEP mathematics average scores for 9-, 13-, and 17-year-old students

These approaches both come with bodies of valid research, but look at existing realities, with a particular focus and set of assumptions. One continues to improve on top-down professional development (PD), and the other documents the reality of its ineffectiveness and acts accordingly. Frankly, I can see the benefit and appeal of both approaches. Yet, these two approaches ultimately lead to frustration over actual teacher adoption rates, flat lined test scores, and wonder why disarming teacher independence has not led to the reform they envision. They provide a narrative that teachers are not changing, yet, from my experience, teachers do change.

Neither approach to understanding teacher learning accounts for how quickly digital slideshows were adopted by teachers - as a core tool in classrooms. Why were these taken up so quickly without directives by the conserving teachers? There are many such examples of technology adoption. Few teachers, for instance, needed workshops on how to use a word processor, or the internet itself, yet thousands of teachers use these tools every day. Video clips effectively and appropriately support teacher lectures and add layers of media to previously audio-dominated practice. This change was an internally driven, widespread, bottom-up, change in practice. Transformation of classroom pedagogical practice may not be as radical as anticipated, but it is also not a benign change when students use, say, digital editors over slate boards. So, if top-down 'training' was not a documented historical impetus for these changes, and teachers still managed to change over time, what did account for mainstream adoption of these tools? What approaches to teacher learning do account for equally interesting realities that teachers sometimes innovate, create, discover, and adopt new classroom practices?

Teachers as Designers

What if we consider the teacher as an artist, or a designer? Some accept that generally teachers *do* adopt new tools and can do so within a short period of time. Consider recent research that documents the teacher as a whole person. They show that teacher beliefs are central to the conversation of technology use and changed practice, (i.e. Ertmer, Ottenbreit-Leftwich, Sadik, Sendurur, & Sendurur, 2012), and that their networks, in and out of the workplace, are essential to their practices (Byrk, A. S., Gomez, L. M. , & Grunow, 2010). These researchers more accurately frame teachers as professional actors within a community of local expertise. For a professional designer, rather than an employee, the decision to change practice is not a lightly made one; it is a locally considered, bottom-up, validation process, using multiple resources to inform practice (Dikkers, 2012). Teachers are essentially independent designers that are unavoidably scanning and searching for improved practices all of the time, but are rooted in designs that have worked in the past. Notably, this approach understands why general core curriculum guides may be welcomed, but specific daily lesson guides are consistently changed or ignored.

This lens treats the teacher as *designer* - a designer with years of developing a thin patience for those that don't understand effective classroom design. Consider that most teachers make micro-changes each time they teach a lesson because they inherently experience student reactions, performances, motivations, disciplines, enthusiasms, and informally collect feedback on lessons each and every hour. They are informed by each iteration to: 1) sustain, 2) tweak, or 3) start over on their designs for each class. Why don't we see sweeping adoption of reforms? Primarily because they are not in conversation with this process. Why do we see teachers embrace some technologies widely? Because some technologies make the design of teaching and learning easier, across subjects, and serve teachers as a blank slate to design as they are inspired.

If teachers are *designers*, (or Teacher-crafters), we can assume that new ideas may not be adopted wholly, but are tested incrementally outside of class, at home, or in small 'free day' activities, before being used as a supplement or single lesson. If this is the case, it is easy to see that formal 'in-service' training really is not all that relevant. Designers want to bounce ideas off of their trusted friends and colleagues before they put work into them. This does not mean that they are 'resistant' to change, it means they are always changing. They are both empowered to ignore top-down training, but not necessarily oriented toward 'conserving' past practice. Quite the opposite actually, a *designer* is naturally seeking the next great idea, new angles, and, as tactics grow expected, the designer seeks to capture student attention with new material. Sometimes teachers like to create something that is their own and see how students react to it. This process is what I call "Teachercraft"; an ongoing process of identifying, validating, experimenting, and appropriating new experiences into the classroom. Using Minecraft then is only a particular kind of Teachercraft.

Why Look at Teachercraft?

If teachers are *designers*, this opens up a new line of questions about how teachers learn and adopt new ideas into their classroom. Why look at teachers? Because in any design field, we should study the innovative designers. For example, if we want to study Impressionism, we do not waste time defining and teaching only the single 'best' Impressionist (via in-service training); nor do we document how they didn't conform to the conventions of the larger French art culture, (and suggest they should have been controlled better); instead we look at each of them as a community of practice and draw actual practice across different styles - understanding what Impressionism is broadly. In the end, we become better educated on the movement of artist-designers.

This is why studying a group of teachers can inform other *designers*, but it may not provide single answers that can be mainstreamed. This book does not provide a bullet point list of how to teach, it does not define a single answer on what innovation is, but it does show a movement of design.

The moment we try to tell an artist the 'right' way to practice, the good artists will keep the profession fresh, new, and give us original material. This can be mistakenly interpreted as 'conserving' or 'resistance'. More accurately, I propose this is the teacher's search for ongoing engagement of an audience that needs original material. In fact, a number of teachers we interviewed for this book have already started looking for the 'next thing' after Minecraft. They are artists, constantly in motion, seeking to get reaction from their students that matches their own enthusiasm for their subject material.

This is why we show common learning tactics, common wisdom and technique, and the common adoption of Minecraft across teachers, but we cannot present a 'best practice' for use of Minecraft in the classroom. A student of the teaching craft, should examine *many* teachers and see each different style as a color contributing to a larger picture of teaching - a movement. Constructivism, for instance, is not 'right', nor is didactic instruction 'wrong', they have both inspired, engaged, and taught children effectively in the hands of *designing* teachers that learn and try new practices. Mastery involves using many tactics, styles, influences, and in time developing your own practice.

If teachers are designers, we should be able to see common tools of the trade, but not common usage of them. We should expect teachers to develop over time, have phases of practice, band together to inform their current interests, and try new things just because the old ones are stale. If teachers are designers, we should be able to ask why they use or do not use classroom technologies and expect robust stories, or narratives, around their decision making process - in truth, there should be a process of design in place.

I assume that teachers are designers. This research carefully examines this process and documents it across cases. If we have the correct theoretical framework, we would expect to see a complex process for evaluating new ideas, a staged experimental process prior to full blown use of Minecraft, and we should expect to see teachers sharing their breakthroughs with refined and complex methods for watching their 'audience' (students), as designers are ultimately interested in how others respond to their design to instruct further iterations on that design.

The next few chapters allow a deeper look at teachers that have already been down the road of trying Minecraft. I will argue that they fit the model of 'designer' as anticipated and the entirety of their communication, across cases, is that of designers, not employees or conservants. Together they paint a picture of what technology adoption looks like in practice for designers. These teachers are, of course, exemplary cases and unique in the profession, but they present evidence that exemplary teachers think of themselves primarily as designers.

Finding Minecraft Teachers

Very quickly[3], with the help of existing Minecraft networks and mailing lists[4], I was able to begin to find and identify teachers that use Minecraft for teaching and learning. As teachers contacted me, I began to filter cases by asking them to share how they used Minecraft in the classroom via e-mail.

Most of the teachers had tried using Minecraft or were just preparing to use it, but I was particularly interested in talking to teachers that were already using Minecraft for: 1) a second (or more) class rotation, 2) across a variety of ages, contexts, and subject areas, and 3) were original in their usage of Minecraft. Thus, of the many educators that responded, seventeen of them stood out as a purposeful sample for learning experience, diversity, and innovation.

---

[3] A formal overview of the study, participant selection, methodology, and analysis will be published separately.

[4] Thank you Joel Levin, GLS, and Mojang!

Participant Educators Using Minecraft for Learning

COUNTRY	SCHOOL	YEARS XP	LEVEL	SUBJECT	GENDER	USE OF MINECRAFT?
Denmark	Alternative	9	HS	English	M	Island
NC, USA	Rural	14	K12	IT	M	State Sites/Open
Australia	Rural	8	HS	Science/Math	M	Community
NY, USA	Urban	10	E/MS	Computer	M	Various
MD, USA	Urban	8	MS	Computer	M	Hunger Games
VT, USA	Rural	19	MS	SocialStudies/ Language Arts	M	Various
Kuwait	Private/Suburb	4	MS	Social Studies	M	World of Humanities
NC, USA	Rural	6	MS	Art	F	Force/Velocity
Australia	Urban	30	K12	Extra-Curr.	F	Sandbox/Free Play
WA, USA	Suburb	-	ES	Extra-Curr.	M	Civics/Free Play
NY, USA	Private/Urban	17	MS	IT	M	Building Ziggurats
Canada	Urban	21	MS	SS/Math/Lang.	M	Math
NJ, USA	Suburb	10	ES	Extra-Curr.	M	Sandbox/Free Play
NJ, USA	Private/Urban	-	ES	Extra-Curr.	F	Sandbox/Free Play
Canada	Urban	5	ES	Language Arts	M	Writing
Canada	Suburb	16	ES	Library	F	Writing
Canada	Urban	10	ES	Library	F	Writing

Thankfully teachers are, in my experience, a sharing, helpful, and generous lot. All seventeen were willing to participate[5] in the full interview process and be identified along with their comments. Most can be found online if you want to compare notes with them too.

---

[5] A small data point that suggests they are neither resistant or stagnant.

Gathering Teacher Stories

With a review board approval and volunteers identified, it was time to talk. I chose to use a narrative analysis approach - used in a previous study of award winning teachers (Dikkers, 2012). This study is an effort to reflect the work of identity psychologist, Dan McAdams, who uses narrative analysis methods to unpack a participants sense of identity, self, and their perception of relevant events. As people develop a sense of self, they remember key narratives, or a 'life story', marked by selected milestones. McAdams shows this expertly in his interview capturing G.W. Bush's (2011) perception of his redemptive self, as data. When people tell stories, they are already selecting stories, from endless non-relevant experiences to expertly filtered relevant ones.

> "The story spells out how you believe you have developed over time and where you think your life is going... Furthermore, much of what we remember relates to our current situation and *future* goals. If I plan to become a physician, I may have very clear memories of learning science and helping people when I was a child."
> (McAdams, 2006, pgs 86-88).

... or, if I am being interviewed about how I can use Minecraft in the classroom, I remember vivid memories of learning Minecraft and share pertinent stories that convey a professional self to the interviewer that is interested in Minecraft.

After preliminary questions and demographic information, I asked participants about their MC use:

- Why you were attracted to MC and how did you begin to use it?
- Talk about your first use of it with kids.
- What results you have seen, and what do you see as the potential of MC for learning?
- What advice do you have for using Minecraft effectively with learners?

These questions were followed up with probing questions to gain clarity on story points. Interviews lasted about forty-five minutes to an hour. I transcribed audio to text and participants were able to read over the interviews and correct, change, or edit any of the content to make sure it read like they meant it. On two occasions, participants used this post-confirmation process to add details.

Though I am not as interested in the self-generating identity of these teachers, I am interested in what they see as key to their development. Their expertise makes their opinions relevant and their stories of learning useful - especially if we see any indication that there are patterns. Across cases, these 'Minecraft stories' may help us to identify both professional development and classroom designs that help you use Minecraft in the classroom. Using narrative analysis provides a method, slightly adopted, to study teacher growth and self-perception of professional development.

Organizing Teacher Stories

After the interviews were concluded, myself and interested graduate students began to read and review the transcriptions and sought out common stories. We proceeded with three reviews, or phases, of analysis:

> Phase 1 - Review and theme building
>
> Phase 2 - Coding data and sorting
>
> Phase 3 - Cross-case analysis

Phase one analysis was to start asking questions of the data to see if there were direct themes. The data pointed to key story elements across teachers. Teachers explained: 1) How they learned about new media technologies; 2) How they validated the use of Minecraft; 3) Design trials and testing efforts they made when they first tried Minecraft; 4) How they refined ideas; and 5) Perceptions of 'best' practices that may work for other teachers.

Phase two used phase one themes to re-read all of the interviews and coded them for stories that answered the questions. We gathered all stories for each theme and built descriptive lists of 'answers' given by teachers, compared lists, and began to make cross-case narratives to be tested in phase three.

Phase three reviewed all data according to themes and looked for patterns and common threads across cases. We also attempted to create common language around the prevalent stories to share them as findings. Coding efforts were to document these stories and accurately 'let the teachers speak for themselves'.

This work is not conclusive, or an indicator of larger populations of teachers, nor should it be. Similar to ethnography, the goal here is to fully understand how these particular teachers learn, grow, and have opinions about using Minecraft. Why look at other teachers? Because they are expert designers and each choice can inspire other designers. This work looks at effective practicing professionals because the work itself is a form of art. The rest of this book, then, is a kind of gallery.

References

Byrk, A. S., Gomez, L. M. , & Grunow, A. (2010). Getting Ideas Into Action: Building Networked Improvement Communities in Education, Carnegie Foundation for the Advancement of Teaching. In C. F. f. t. A. o. Teaching (Ed.), *Carnegie Perspectives*. Stanford, CA: Creative Commons.

Cox, Andrew. (2005). What are communities of practice? A comparative review of four seminal works. Journal of Information Science, 31(6), 527-540. doi: 10.1177/0165551505057016.

Cuban, L., & Cuban, L. (2009). *Oversold and underused: Computers in the classroom.* Harvard University Press.

Desimone, L. M. . (2011). A primer on effective professional development. Phi Delta Kappan, 92(6), 68-71.

Dikkers, S. (2012). *The Professional Development Trajectories of Teachers successfully integrating and practicing with New Information and Communication Technologies.* (PhD), University of Wisconsin - Madison, Ann Arbor Retrieved from http://search.proquest.com/docview/1033501351 (3513241).

Elmore, R. F. (2000). *Building a new structure for school leadership* (pp. 1-46). Washington, DC: Albert Shanker Institute.

Ertmer, Peggy A., Ottenbreit-Leftwich, Anne T., Sadik, Olgun, Sendurur, Emine, & Sendurur, Polat. (2012). Teacher Beliefs and Technology Integration Practices: A Critical Relationship. *Computers & Education, 59*(2), 423-435.

McAdams, Dan P. (2011). *George W. Bush and the redemptive dream : a psychological portrait.* Oxford ; New York: Oxford University Press.

McAdams, Dan P., Josselson, Ruthellen, & Lieblich, Amia. (2006). *Identity and story : creating self in narrative* (1st ed.). Washington, DC: American Psychological Association.

Postman, N. (1979). Teaching as a conserving activity. *Instructor, 89*(4).

CHAPTER 5

HOW DO TEACHERS VALIDATE THE USE OF MINECRAFT?

"Then, the final nail in the coffin that convinced me
how much benefit there was is that she learned how to spell
her first word because of Minecraft."

- Minecraft Teacher

Validating Validation

Minecraft use may be a promising idea to you, but you may not be ready to use Minecraft in the classroom quite yet. Or, you are hearing a lot about other teachers using Minecraft and want to know more. It may be that your students are very excited about Minecraft and gave you a copy of this book! If so, you are in a process of *validation* that is consistently part of every Minecraft-for-learning teacher narrative. Validation is the process of moving from *hearing*, about a new practice, tool, or idea for the classroom, to *using* it for teaching and learning. Consistently, teachers need a time to think about and see a path for appropriating new ideas for classroom use prior to actual use.

This chapter defines, across cases, what this validation process includes among exemplary and innovative teachers. Interestingly, these teachers learned new practices quickly, efficiently, and effectively using their lifetime interests, talking with students, and leveraging online resources to inform their practice.

The current and widespread belief about professional development (PD) is that if a teacher is told convincingly about a promising classroom idea, that they return to their classroom and try it. Summative literature outlines "core features", for formal PD, including a presentation that has a "focus on content, active learning, coherence, duration, and collective participation" (Desimone, 2011). Where this literature is well established, *none* of the teachers (n=17) in this study were fully convinced to use Minecraft because of a single workshop or presentation. Which begs the question, if they were not *taught* to use Minecraft, how did they learn?

When asked, *"Where did you first hear about Minecraft?"*, our teachers actually describe multiple experiences including informal and digitally mediated experiences. They explain transformative informal professional development elements that appear consistently across cases. This chapter reviews past work that similarly finds these informal learning elements to be central to exemplary teacher growth, identifies what the resources are using the teachers' own words, and suggests how to build your own PD program toward exemplary practices.

Exemplary Teacher Professional Development

Full disclosure, I had every reason to ask about validation in this study. Two years ago I was studying award winning, or 'exemplary', teachers about how they came into their current practices. These participants included Teachers of the Year, the ING Innovators, Presidential Award winners, and others (n=32). I wondered if the exemplary teachers learned the way the primers said they do, or if they had innovative PD strategies that led to innovative teaching? What was their 'trajectory of learning'? What was their story? This study and the current Minecraft teachers used the same narrative approach (Dikkers, 2012).

My hypothesis was that as the flow of information shifted to digital mediums, so would the professional development; that teachers may not need to wait on the next workshop to hop online, meet other teachers, and find ideas for lesson planning. In the same ways that information and communication were speeding up other professions, teaching PD was silently undergoing a revolution of its own. Among our awarded teachers, at least, it was.

First, I learned that not all award-winning teachers reacted to formal PD the same way. In fact, some did tell stories that included formal PD as relevant to their growth (29%) - this included a good 'in-service' training session, project group, learning community, or conference session. But more often teachers gave conditional (39%) or negative (24%) answers that formal PD was a hit-or-miss endeavor; commonly:

> "We would count the light bulb in the ceiling while the person goes on
> and on" (p.121)

Teachers pointed this out even when not directly asked, because it was key to their storytelling to point out that they took a 'new' path to learning. At best, for the sampling, formal strategies are inconsistently effective. And when they positively pointed out the benefits, they shifted to extra-curricular tasks.

> "They are helpful to me to make sure the kids get on the bus the right way,
> but not for anything in the classroom" (p. 122)

For expert teachers, as good as the PD might have been once, there were now other sources of training and development that were consistently more relevant to them and part of their narrative toward award winning practice.

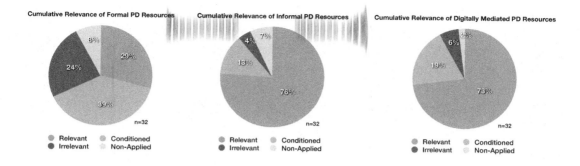

Though this study captured that teachers were learning elsewhere, I did not see the pattern soon enough to dedicate interview time to specifically probe on exactly how this happened. What did convince them that an idea was worth trying in the classroom? How did they validate a new practice? This study built forward and teachers were able to share their recent memories of validations. Teachers explained that they 1) learn from their lives, 2) validate with their students, and 3) build on knowledge using digitally mediated resources.

Learning from Their Lives

Teachers told their stories and highlighted mostly informal activities (71%) that moved them from *hearing* to *use*. Remarkably, these narratives were filled with PD examples like hobbies, trying things at home, experimenting in class, student ideas, learning/playing informally with students, surfing the net, and community groups.

A sampling:

> "Fly fishing... it has informed my classroom..."
>
> "I read, I do yoga and that influences..."
>
> "My pilot training plays a big effect in me..."
>
> "Parenting"
>
> "Reading and travel..."

and leading into this study,

> "I was attracted to Minecraft when I saw students playing it during their breaks."

Broadly spoken, teachers were always on the lookout for new ideas,

> "Every single thing I do, every single thing..."
>
> "That's what I do... I'm always looking...".

Indeed, this data looked less like the PD primers, and more like Jenkins (2009) participatory cultures; or Ito's (2010) 'hanging out' and 'messing around'; or Steinkuehler's (2006) 'third spaces'. This cannot be understated. Every single participant in that study (100%) named a personal interest or hobby as relevant resources for their teaching practice, growth, and professional development. Even with only 32 teachers, that leads to a compelling commonality among our awarded teachers, why wasn't there more research around teacher interests?

These teachers did not necessarily follow the PD learning patterns expected of employees; they were much more like designers. Hobbies consistently stood out in the narratives as inspirational elements and creative teachers were looking everywhere for new ideas. This was worth pursuing. If this is the case, then when we focus on Minecraft, will there be more common sources that lead to the particular tool?

Validation from Their Students

A second common finding was the central importance of the students themselves. Award-winning teachers learned from their students,

> "Not once in a while, all the time. All the time."

Similarly universal conditions introduced these kinds of student stories in the narratives (italics are mine),

> "Students are the greatest source"
>
> "*Constantly* teaching me things";
>
> "I get feedback from my kids *all the time*";
>
> "Students *always* drive what you do,... if you watch them enough".

To these teachers, students are completely central to innovation and practice. This cannot be understated. Teachers tested everything against student reactions, behaviors, and learning. Before they ran with an idea they would verbally run it past students over lunch break or after school, test it in an after school setting, or run a single hour version of it - solely to see how students would react.

Minecraft, likewise, was enthusiastically presented to teachers in this study. Students were consistently part of the stories, and even were presented as the initial starting points for teachers.

"My initial experience with Minecraft came through students. Students introduced me to Minecraft. Actually, not students that I was directly involved with in the school system but indirectly involved with or played World of Warcraft with outside of school."

As with the award winning teachers, the 10 out of 17 Minecraft teachers noted either playing with children at home, showing it to students at school, or both:

"So, [I discovered Minecraft] playing with my daughter, in school I'd pull one or two kids over to my desk and say what do you think of this game. What do you think of the graphics? I thought a lot of kids would be turned off by the simplistic graphics but quite the opposite. They were intrigued."

Both studies confirmed a pattern of reacting to student feedback around new ideas in the classroom.

Digitally Mediated Learning

Exemplary teachers also learned from digitally mediated resources. Though the teachers weren't selected for their use of technology in particular, when asked how they learned, they consistently named online communities, videos, information/idea sources, tools, and video gaming. A rough mapping of these stories across the interviews, and coded for the context of the story (relevant, neutral, or irrelevant to their learning) shows a clear pattern of how important online resources are to exemplary teachers.

This finding led to the Minecraft study. Instead of pursuing how to make formal PD better, it seemed obvious that informal and digitally mediated teacher learning would be much more interesting and essential. Something was enabling these teachers to move from idea to practice. Minecraft is one of these online resources. How exactly did they validate using it in class?

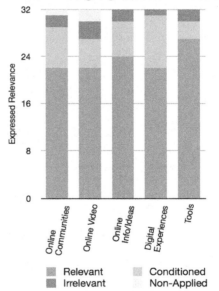

Relevance of Digitally Mediated PD Resources

	Online Communities	Online Video	Online Info/Ideas	Digital Experiences	Tools
Relevant	22	22	24	22	27
Conditioned	7	5	6	9	3
Irrelevant	2	3	2	1	2
Non-Applied	1	2	0	0	0

Elements that Validate Minecraft for Teaching and Learning

Teachers using Minecraft were selected in part because of their use of this tool. Naturally then, all of the participants (n=17) shared narratives describing how they discovered, saw potential, and decided to try using Minecraft. Teachers explained that they needed multiple elements to convince them to use Minecraft. Interestingly, not one teacher had a single experience that led to using Minecraft; instead, validation narratives contained anywhere between two to seven elements, but most (n=10) contained four to five elements, and averaged 4.49 elements per participant. Seven of the teachers explained that at one point they actually said, "No" to Minecraft at one point in the validation process.

PD elements were limited to only seven named within these narratives. Participants listed seven types of validation elements. Here is a closer look:

#	ELEMENT OF VALIDATION	NUMBER OF PARTICIPANTS NAMING ELEMENTS	% OF PARTICIPANTS NAMING ELEMENT	TOTAL # OF TIMES NAMED
1	Playing Minecraft personally	16	94%	17
2	Gaming as a hobby	15	88%	16
3	Online information and communities	10	59%	15
4	Friend's recommendation	7	41%	7
5	Enthusiasm of students at school	7	41%	8
6	Watching a child at home	6	35%	7
7	Conference	4	24%	4

All but one teacher had to play the games themselves (1) as part of their journey (Chapter 3!). Others had used other games in their classrooms and approached Minecraft more ready to see it as a valid resource (2). Each element provided a contact point for the teacher to hear about Minecraft and/or hear others praise it as an educational tool.

One participant coded all seven in their story about choosing to use Minecraft in the classroom. Prior to a final decision to use, this teacher shares a rapid fire collection of stories that led him to using Minecraft. No one single element made this happen. Significant and complex validation 'work' is being done prior to formal classroom application and usage. This teacher, in particular, required multiple positive elements to overcome an initial rejection of Minecraft and develop an awareness of it as an interesting tool. As a veteran teacher he has a growing conviction that Minecraft has potential (especially watching his daughter over time) and that his students at school would welcome an opportunity to learn with Minecraft. His telling:

"I came across it very, very early on. It was before it was even an alpha. I don't even think it had a name. It was just sort of this experimental game that this guy called Notch was working on…" (Gaming as a Hobby)

"…I saw it on a game discussion forum and I tried the free version and I got on a multi-player server, my first experience was on a multi-player and it was just this really chaotic world… I thought, 'Oh, that's interesting,' but I sort of discounted it. I said this is not for me…" (Online community)

"…Then it was probably a good sixth months later I was at Quakecon 2010 and… In fact, it was sort of the underground hit of Quakecon 2010 and if you know, they have very large LAN so there are several thousand people with their computers all networked together and everywhere you looked there were people playing Minecraft either by themselves or multi-player…" (Conference)

"…A friend said have you played Minecraft? It's really great. I said, I've seen it and it's not for me. He said, no, no, look at it. It has really evolved. At this point, the game had a survival mode. It was in a natural landscape and there was a large adventure component and creation component and I dove right in… and my very first thought is gee my daughter would love to play this game…"
(Friend's Recommendation)

"… She was almost five at the time, lets just say 4 1/2 and I thought she would like to explore and be able to build houses and I didn't know quite what she would want to do. I didn't think she'd be able to play by herself. I figured very often when we play she would sit on my lap and I'd play the game and she'd tell me what to do, that kind of thing. So, when I came home, I think I described it as the world game to her because every time you played, the game created a new world to explore and she loved it and every single day it was, 'Daddy, let's play the world game.' (Playing Minecraft Personally)

"…At first, she just liked cutting down trees and building little wooden houses. She wanted me to turn the monsters off because they were too scary but then I was a very proud dad when one day she said, 'Daddy, I think maybe you could turn the monsters on but keep them on easy mode… Then, the final nail in the coffin that convinced me how much benefit there was is that she learned how to spell her first word because of Minecraft. She wanted to be able to teleport herself back to her home in the game and I had set up that if you typed /home you'd teleport home so she came up to me one day and asked me how to spell home and that was the first word she ever learned to spell."
(Watching a Child at Home - full cuteness)

"...So, as I was playing with her, I had it in the back of my mind that my second grade students specifically, I thought, would get a lot out of this... ... In school I'd pull one or two kids over to my desk and say 'What do you think of this game'? What do you think of the graphics? I thought a lot of kids would be turned off by the simplistic graphics but quite the opposite. They were intrigued. They had never seen a game like this and were very, very curious. All of this really gave me the confidence to dive in and create a little unit about Minecraft." *(Enthusiasm of students at School)*

Needing the least amount of validation (3 elements), another teacher had a history of gaming and immediately saw potential in Minecraft. Later however, he added that he had tried out the game with his kids at home and at school.

" I played, I am a gamer, I've been a gamer all my life and so I was gaming at the time playing World of Warcraft...and it [Minecraft] was so different and so I played it...it was such a different game and I was just getting into teaching and using other video games with kids. I immediately thought this would be absolutely amazing to used with students because it is a captivating game that doesn't have all the things that normally exclude off the shelf games from being used in schools." *(Gaming as a Hobby)*

"When it comes to using it with kids... I also started using it with my own two children as well as with my students so I have both of those lenses on when when I think about using it with kids." *(Watching a child at home + Enthusiasm of students at school)*

Playing Minecraft and *Gaming as a Hobby* was most common with Minecraft users as only two of the participants did not mention previous game play or hobby time with digital communities as relevant to their validation of Minecraft. In these two cases a good friend was involved that was a gamer. It should also be noted that when conferences were mentioned, it was often in regards to meeting people at conferences, not necessarily attending a particular session or lecture.

On occasion, the teacher would include two or more specific instances of an element influencing their validation. Of note is *Online Information and Communities* where participants reported multiple and distinct stories about different online sources. The data does not capture the number of sites, conversations, and videos that were watched during these times, only that the participant named this as a relevant part of their learning, so even the number of elements recorded may not represent the detail with which they spent time online learning and gathering ideas.

Knowing the number of occurring elements is not the full picture however. These elements were always found in combination with each other. The following data shows the chronological ordering of these elements for each teacher. When a teacher mentioned previous experience, for instance, with game play, as a relevant part of their story, these were located prior to when participants were 'aware' of Minecraft. Normally however, most told their stories in chronological progressions.

Below, bold italic lettering identifies when participants rejected Minecraft (n=8). Also, italic identifies the point at which teachers saw potential for Minecraft to be used in classrooms (-->). Bold lettering (n=9) shows that the teacher had previously used digitally mediated learning (DML) in the classroom, legitimizing games for learning.

Narrated Order of Elements of Validation

KEY: **DML History**	***Rejects Minecraft***	*Sees Potential*					
PARTICIPANTS	**PREVIOUS GAME HISTORY**	**1ST AWARE OF MINECRAFT**					**USE OF MINECRAFT**
1	2			5	7	3	1 ⟶
2	2	5	***3***	3	5		1 ⟶
3		4		*3*	1		3 ⟶
4	2	3	***1***	4	7	6	5 ⟶
5	2	1					1 ⟶
6	2	3	***1***				6 ⟶
7	2		***3***	*3*	1		3 ⟶
8	2			4			1 ⟶
9	2	5	***1***	*3*	3	4	1 ⟶
10	2	1					1 ⟶
11	2		***1***	4	*1*	3	6 ⟶
12			***6***	6	*1*		5 ⟶
13	2		***4***	5			1 ⟶
14	2	3		6	5		1 ⟶
15	2	3					1 ⟶
16	2			4			7 ⟶
17	2			7	4	6	1 ⟶

1) Playing Minecraft personally; 2) Gaming as a hobby; 3) Online information and communities; 4) Friend's recommendation; 5) Enthusiasm of students at school; 6) Watching a child at home; and 7) Conference.

Commonly teachers gamed as a hobby and brought this into the classroom, but it was not always the case that they had to play the game themselves before deciding to use Minecraft for learning.

Did veteran users of DML require less validation? No, the number of elements needed to validate did not significantly change when a teacher had previous experience using digitally mediated experiences in class. Of the seventeen participants, eight claimed to be using a digital environment (of any type) in the classroom for the first time with Minecraft. Nine, 'veterans', had previous experience using digitally mediated environments for classroom learning (including Second Life, World of Warcraft, River City, Wolfquest, Pokemon, Webkins, and Quest Atlantis). In addition, validation was not apparently related to years teaching or context of practice. In other words, we had a good mix of new and veteran games for learning teachers in the study. Nor did being a veteran simplify the process of validation.

The veteran gaming teachers still required an average of 4.44 elements to validate use, and the 'newbies' shared slightly fewer elements (4.25) and they both had a range of two to seven elements. The previous use of digital experiences did not show significant difference in the number of elements needed to validate Minecraft for classroom. Likewise years of teacher practice had no significant effect on validation elements.

Along each of the narrative plot lines, teachers described a point at which they 'got it', or saw that Minecraft could be used for the classroom ('Potential') - even if they didn't quite know how to use it. It was at this point that the teacher would start to pursue ideas, examples, and explanations of using Minecraft for learning. On six occasions, seeing potential led directly to trials in the classroom. Preceding elements were distributed between playing Minecraft personally, seeing something online, a friend, student enthusiasm, and watching a child play Minecraft at home.

#	ELEMENT OF VALIDATION	NUMBER OF TIMES PRECEDING 'POTENTIAL'	% NAMING ELEMENT AS 'POTENTIAL'	# OF TIMES PRECEDING 'USE'	% NAMING ELEMENT AS 'USE'
1	Playing Minecraft personally	5	29%	10	59%
2	Gaming as a hobby	0	0%	0	0%
3	Online information and communities	3	18%	2	12%
4	Friend's recommendation	2	12%	0	0%
5	Enthusiasm of students at school	3	18%	2	12%
6	Watching a child at home	4	24%	2	12%
7	Conference	0	0%	1	6%

Prior to 'Potential', teachers were receiving elements, afterwards they would pursue elements of validation toward the use of Minecraft in the classroom ('Use'). Personal play time was the compelling element that led to actual use of Minecraft for most of the participants (n=10). For some, the choice to use was simple:

> "I got an email from her saying I know this guy called Liam who is awesome and he wants to do this thing with Minecraft. I don't know what it is but want to try? I said, yeah, I want to do a PLC that is formalized and I said yes I'm in."

For others, seeing the potential was harder. Half of the eight participants that rejected Minecraft initially were basing this decision on playing the game themselves. Personal play of Minecraft was the most significant factor in making pedagogical choices about not using Minecraft too.

> "After taking a look at some of the videos on the website and kind of examine the game I essentially laughed and said, 'No way looking at the graphics... you've got to be kidding me,' and then went back to playing World of Warcraft."

To overcome rejection of the idea, teachers needed to personally use Minecraft *again* in all but two of the cases, where it took seeing a child play at home to convince the teacher of the learning potential of Minecraft.

When presented with a compelling technology, teachers need to play the game for themselves prior to making the decision to try it in the classroom - often more than once. Over half of the time this was the element that directly precedes the choice to use Minecraft in the classroom. On two occasions, teachers only needed one element (in addition to being lifetime gamers) to validate classroom use - both times this was personal play. Within this sample, the time to personally test-drive Minecraft was the most powerful and common validation asset.

Finally, in the cases where hobby participation led to awareness, teachers had to play for themselves to see if it had potential in the classroom - even in the cases where these were the only two elements narrated. Playing Minecraft personally was the most common cause of seeing potential, and choosing to try Minecraft in the classroom.

Using Elements of Validation as Professional Support

Validation is often overlooked, but in these cases it shows an important aspect of teacher growth toward using digital media in classrooms. These narratives show validation as essential starting points for teacher innovation. Prior to accepting an idea or planning for classroom use of Minecraft, *all* of the teachers in this study expressed a narrative, with four to five elements, that led to validating the idea and ultimately transforming their classrooms.

Most of these teachers needed to try Minecraft out, even if it meant rejecting it at first, then continue to hear and learn more about it. All too often, anything less than compliance with formal PD strategies marks the teacher as 'stubborn', 'resistant', or 'coasting toward retirement'. The result is a misperception of the modern teacher that doesn't want to try innovative strategies in the classroom.

Worse, single-element PD potentially assumes that teachers are willing to let 'experts' validate an idea without local discernment. Thinking that a single session or book on an idea, (no matter the degree of fidelity to design), will transform teacher practice or even validate the potential of an idea is simply not supported by this data. This doesn't take into account a natural and positive process of validation that is evident when we take a closer look at innovative teaching. This process is locally relevant, involved, ongoing, and complex - and this small study only identifies its presence, not the full range of its workings. In short, I propose that a stronger appreciation for the validation process would paint a different picture of the modern teacher - or at the least, we should be thankful these teachers put so much consideration into design prior to use.

Notice that 'seeing potential' was separate from 'choosing to use' Minecraft for learning in the teacher-design process. In fact, the two are distinct and separate in most cases. We saw this when trying Mobile Media Learning (Dikkers, Martin, & Coulter, 2012) models with teachers too. Initially we would provide a game intervention that teachers would praise in the post-interviews, but then note that they would never try it out on their own. Seeing the potential of mobile learning was a positive stage, but the challenges of using new technology without researcher support, was still unaddressed for the teachers. 'Believing in' and 'acting on' are clearly different parts of validation.

If these are indeed separated for the larger population of teachers, then we need to plan accordingly when designing professional development interventions or presenting new pedagogical practices to teachers. Consider personal exposure (play), lifetime hobbies (learning), and online information (inquiry) as the most commonly involved stories of validation. These three elements may actually be *more* affordable, convenient, and deliverable than traditional, formal strategies. For our teachers, they are clearly more impactful. What if these were elements that school leaders actively tried to encourage? How would it affect teaching and learning in your school?

Time to Play

Personally trying out Minecraft was, most commonly, the final step prior to a decision to try it in the classroom. Hands on testing can be as affordably organized as an in-service presentation. Instead of presenting an idea, for instance, PD designers should consider showing design potential and use to teachers; alongside letting teachers try something out for themselves and with their children at home or at school. 'Show, don't tell', applies to adult learners too - and it should be assumed that one element will not result in changed classroom practices.

Districts that expect any technology integration without allowing teachers to take home that technology and 'play with it', should expect marked detachment from the creative design process of classroom planning. Without time to explore and consider, the new tools or applications simply are not present as teachers think of new ideas and projects for next week. With a modest amount of planning, providing teachers with new technology a year ahead of any formal expectations could align with the findings here and potentially have a greater chance to result in innovative teaching than a presentation alone would. In short, buy teachers toys to play with, let them take the new technology home, and pilot test use prior to large scale adoption. This tip alone could save millions, nationally, in technology purchases. If teachers cannot design for use in their classrooms, save your district a stunning amount of money, and wait until teachers do have particular technologies they want for teaching and learning.

Promoting and sharing interesting and compelling classroom trials (even imperfect ones) would also promote the design-focus that teachers like thrive within. Consider starting, ending, or filling staff meetings with faculty sharing their most recent efforts for engaging learning design. Put a spotlight on playful design efforts, 'plan B's, and cheer success along with... initiative.

Learning Everywhere

At first glance, hobbies are hard to encourage. We can even ask if we should seek too. In fact, if teachers are just employees, it may not be appropriate to encourage any activities outside of work. Minecraft teachers were not necessarily going to Minecraft communities until they saw potential in the software - however many were already in video game communities. So if teachers are designers, sharing and celebrating any activities of excellence is actually supporting and condoning hobbies, or more appropriately, high interest, lifetime learning habits. Initially, professional learning communities (PLCs) were promoted with similar evidence that innovation commonly started in trusted conversation. However, when these were mandated, and often organized by grade or subject, they lost their potency to influence active, vibrant, teacher learning.

Promoting lifetime learning may still be within reach. PLCs could easily be arranged around high interest areas like computer gaming, civic engagement, project-based learning, and new topics could be driven by teacher suggestion. This data shows that these groups may not naturally form around grade levels or subject areas, but informally gather around common interests. Teachers can easily translate a science teachers use of Minecraft for use in their history lessons. Also, they are only, ever, one of seven elements found in this study and not all teachers came to innovative practice because of a community. PLC groups should be highly enjoyable, fluid, and voluntary.

For education leaders, showing interest, and modeling, participation in clubs, community groups, volunteer activities, and online communities can serve to show younger teachers how these are relevant activities. Willfully choose to tune into new ideas and tune out empty small talk. When a respected (valid) leader chooses to focus conversation on lifetime learning, it sets a bar for professionals to get involved, geek out, and play - just to be more interesting to their colleagues. Consider gently starting in the interview process and continue by bringing it up in annual merit conversations to sustain a culture that legitimizes passionate investment in hobbies and new skills.

Learning with and from students is a form of learning everywhere. In the cases of our Minecraft teachers, the students were often the 'experts' that teachers leaned on for initial classroom efforts. Designing teachers actively sought out feedback from students and based key decisions on their reactions to an idea. Little attention is given to training teachers for this kind of data, yet we see consistently that innovative teachers measure each effort by student reactions. Techniques for gathering student feedback are easy to teach, model, and highlight in formal training.

Recently we've also had great success involving student presenters at our local Playful Learning Summit and working with student teams as personal coaches for teachers that are taking their first steps in digital environments. Students have been consistently excited to show teachers new tools, they are patient, and they are familiar with coaching others to play.

Supporting Online Literacy

Finally, districts can easily provide links, leads, and provide guidance for using the internet as an information and community building asset. When a teacher is interested in using Minecraft in the classroom, a district can dedicate attention to saving the teacher time looking for more information, people, and examples of use.

For example, the drive to have local 'data-based decision making' may be well received as having the potential to improve learning, but teachers and administrators also *need tools to process student data* in a timely, effective, and even exploratory way. For data to affect daily choices it most likely has to fit within the constraints of time, cost, ability, comfort, and safety that are also part of teacher decision making. These are all based on a person's competency and knowledge base around digital tools. Supporting online resources means building tools, communications, and support for teachers so they can efficiently and effectively do things for themselves.

It is worth reasserting that the prevalence of informal PD around new media technologies can easily be explained by the newness of the technologies. We simply haven't formalized training yet. So, conditionally, this study (and the limits of both the sampling and method) should not be used as a critique of formal PD, only that informal PD is currently prevalent for new technology adopters. Formal PD may in the future address the need to build teacher capacity using online tools - moving from boutique to mainstream practices.

Conclusion

Understanding a process of validation provides a new lens through which we can look at teachers and how they actually validate and adopt Minecraft in their classrooms. Teachers are essential designers constantly looking for and validating old and new practices. As information is digitized, it stands to reason that teacher validation elements are shifting toward both digital resources and communities of practice that can expand and filter ideas for new classroom practices. Second, I'm convinced that a better understanding of how teachers design their practice can open up new conversations about structuring PD more effectively. If teachers naturally leverage informal PD assets, then formal PD designers can potentially also benefit from appropriately updating new PD designs that more naturally fit with evidence of actual adult learning.

Personal play, having a hobby (related to the intervention), student reactions, and personal relationships (friends and colleagues) were all key elements that contributed to a clear process of validation prior to adoption of Minecraft. Validation, though varied, was consistently communicated through narrative as a process of moving from aware of Minecraft, to seeing potential in Minecraft, to choosing to try using Minecraft in the classroom. Next, we have the privilege in hearing how those first efforts played out, how the ideas were refined, and how they ended up with their current practices.

References

Desimone, L. M. (2011). A primer on effective professional development. *Phi delta kappan, 92*(6), 68-71.

Dikkers, S., Martin, J., Coulter, B. (2012). *Mobile media learning : Amazing uses of mobile devices for learning.* Pittsburgh, PA: ETC Press.

Dikkers, S. (2012). *The Professional Development Trajectories of Teachers successfully integrating and practicing with New Information and Communication Technologies.* (PhD), University of Wisconsin - Madison, Ann Arbor Retrieved from http://search.proquest.com/docview/1033501351 (3513241)

Itō, Mizuko. (2010). *Hanging out, messing around, and geeking out : kids living and learning with new media.* Cambridge, Mass.: MIT Press.

Jenkins, Henry. (2009). *Confronting the challenges of participatory culture : media education for the 21st century.* Cambridge, Mass.: MIT Press.

Steinkuehler, C. A., & Williams, D. (2006). Where everybody knows your (screen) name: Online games as "third places". *Journal of Computer Mediated Communication, 11*(4), 885-909.

CHAPTER 6

HOW DO TEACHERS USE MINECRAFT OUTSIDE OF CLASSROOMS?

Zack Gilbert and Seann Dikkers

"Within two days, we had 120 kids sign up so we blew through the requirements and had more sign ups for the program than any other topic ever offered by the school in its twenty year history."
- Minecraft Teacher

The Petri Dish Club

Validating a tool like Minecraft is closely tied to working 'with' and 'for' students. Likewise after our teachers made the decision to use Minecraft, eleven of them chose to organize, (or let students organize!), a club *outside* of their classrooms and their narratives pause to elaborate and emphasize how instrumental these experiences were for them. For our teachers, outside of class time with learners was essentially a kind of petri dish for cultivating and growing new ideas.

We too will spend a chapter unpacking why teachers choose to organize 'clubs', what they think about that time, and how they begin to tie emergent activities into classroom learning experiences. Outside of class time also serves to train the teacher, provide ideas, and allow a natural process of testing, organizing, and developing group management around a piece of software. Broadly, understanding why and how teachers build clubs is an essential aspect of understanding professional learning processes.

This chapter first reviews narrative insights provided by our 17 Minecraft teachers and the end of the chapter includes a step by step guide to starting your own Minecraft club. Guest writer Zack Gilbert brings his experience explaining how he thinks about and goes about planning for a new club. First though we will explore why you might want to invest the time to start a club.

Why Start a Club?

Across the narratives in this study, teachers spend time explaining why they felt it was important, or essential to them, to start a Minecraft club. Clubs, in general, are good because they provide a safe space, build community, provide common ground for students, challenge them, and they are fun. Together, Minecraft teachers added their own professional development, lesson ideas, digital literacy, balance, and escape from curricular goals as core reasons why they invested time into meeting with kids outside of class.

Our teachers started explaining how important it is to try things out in a club first. Notably, for non-gaming teachers, playing in a play space helps them to learn the 'language' of gaming without the burden of curricular goals. To this end, knowing gaming terms, styles of play, student interest, basic mechanics, and rhythms of play are a form of literacy worth getting more familiar with as a teacher.

> "As games explode and become the cool thing that a lot of teachers want to try out they all just think that they can… not all, but many, and they don't have any background… you need to know the language of it. I think teachers can bring so much as long as they are approaching it from a gamer point of view or lens."

> "I think teachers have to learn to get out of the way and let the kids play the games and see where they can fit the learning in. Once teachers start trying to cram the learning into the game, you will kill the game and the game won't be fun."

If they are not, teachers are prone to colonize the game space with goals, assignments and forced actions that may not fit with what is fun (and compelling) about the game itself. This particular teacher went on to explain that teachers who aren't familiar with digital environments tend to 'assign' work and tasks that are out of alignment with the tool. This can actually have an adverse effect, rendering the tool powerless for learning. It is essential to make time to be able to watch students and integrate, not take over, learning spaces. Other teachers take time, without playing themselves, to see student actions and behaviors outside of the classroom:

> "We took a little time to think what could we do with this and how could we use it and to come up with ideas… The more I saw, the more I realized what you could do. I admit I probably have only played it 10 minutes myself."

> "The whole jumping into the game and not really knowing how to play the game is actually part of the game and part of the fun because they start out and a lot of them don't even know how to walk… So, I think the best advice I can give is to just jump into it."

Where teacher playtime varies between the teachers, they are essentially all seeking the same thing outside of class. They are trying to negotiate how the digital tools can be used, how they should be used, how their goals and the goals of the players can be balanced between learning and play.

> "I still try when I'm creating a new activity to find that balance, to give them a sense of purpose, to give them a goal but also include segments of game play where you are just playing Minecraft."

Another reason for starting an informal club for students is to escape the need to justify time spent. Classroom time essentially is set aside for learning a curriculum. Teachers, arguably, need to be able to explain each lesson and how they expect it to lead to learning. Currently, efforts to evaluate and quantify 'value-added' puts even more pressure on ensuring each moment in class serves the curricular goal.

> "I have curriculum to deliver and assessment to do and recording to get done. I can not just let them play. I don't know if that is short sightedness on me or whether that is just a fact."

Yet outside of class…

> "That argument can't hold up against when it is extracurricular, when it's enrichment, and supplemental, and we're still doing exactly what we've done before in the classroom."

Moving outside the classroom, then, is a clever way to experiment with new learning tools, without having to explain them. Often teachers will see the relevance of digital media in the classroom and ask where to start making changes to their classes. For these teachers, the answer is to leave the classroom alone and get to know Minecraft outside of classes.

Another small benefit to outside of class exposure was shared by one teacher that had tried classroom adoption first, and then saw the benefit of training a small, highly interested, cohort of players first, then bringing the game to the classroom.

> "I tell you what the first two weeks where you are trying to teach 15 plus students at a time how to play a game, that may or may not have had experience with computer games, that is awful. However, it pays off. As soon as they learn how to play, then they start teaching each other and then it gets much easier."

Similarly, using Minecraft outside of the classroom allows a teacher that is not technologically savvy to gain knowledge. For teachers that are new to games, virtual environments, or managing a classroom with computer users, this can be a safe place to learn and understand.

"I mean it doesn't have to be as big of a thing as I've made it for my kids. It can just be a day a month or something like that, where maybe the teacher doesn't understand as much about it technologically but can run it in the classroom, but just open to… reaching students who have a variety of learning styles."

"I don't know enough about how these kids will react to the game so I really felt it made sense to start with something that was really close to the original Minecraft experience."

Our teachers also explain that they organize time outside of class because it fulfills them. This is not necessarily new, teachers have coached, advised, and opened up their classrooms after school for decades because kids can just be fun to spend time with - especially around a high interest activity.

"It is really fun to have these big epic wins with the students. I feel like it has made me a much happier teacher."

These weren't the *most* important reason why to start a club however. Most commonly, playing with students served as a petri dish for understanding how to use the tool itself. Teachers explained that they would invite the kids in, step back, and watch them. Their advice is to relax, play, and spend more time with the people that love and embrace the software. As a teacher, with expertise in the content areas, you should be able to see natural fits between the tool and your curriculum.

"Having the teachers not be afraid to fail in a club is good. Failure is okay for teachers and students. When teachers feel pressure to teach the prescribed curriculum, failure seems to be a time waster, when in many cases it leads to deeper understanding."

The theme of failure carries over into classroom use also, but those teachers that started a club explained clearly that informal spaces allowed them to try more unique and experiential learning ideas without the pressure to cover content - until they were adequately convinced that the informal learning space presented results that measured up to their expectations in the classroom.

Stepping Back

Stepping back is actually a strategy for professional learning. Teachers explain how relevant and important it is to simply watch students. To these teachers, this process is a starting point, not an evaluation of new ideas. Instead of generating a great lesson idea and testing it, they start by stepping back.

"One of the first things... is to allocate some time to just see what the kids do."

"We were just going to see exactly the kids could do with this game and what direction they wanted to take it in and what direction we wanted to take it in."

"Working in these virtual spaces over the past few years, I have discovered the best way to develop robust programs is... simply playing with the kids BEFORE creating curriculum."

Notice the goal for the teacher in this space is to watch, listen, and learn. Consistently teachers sought to communicate how important it was to approach new tools by enjoying them and letting ideas come naturally. In this sense, the teachers role is to actively and purposefully enjoy a game first.

We also see teacher framing their role as one of supporting the player goals, or helping students to fully enjoy the game:

"I'm mostly just watching the girls and seeing what they do and what they like to do and then trying to help them be successful at it."

"We took a view of stepping back to see where kids would take this sandbox if they were in control of it and so our role in the space was to... support them in what they would like to do with the server..."

Stepping back is not a passive activity. Observation of students playing Minecraft is a fast track into expert design. "Notice that what these teachers often condition as "stepping back" is actually a significant learning activity for the them. This is much more relevant than they make it out to be. First, notice that they are choosing to tell these stories as part of a larger narrative on how they came to use Minecraft. "Just watching", then, is relevant enough a year or two later to share in a formal interview setting. Second, notice that their work after "just" is very specific; they "see exactly" what students do, what their preferences are, and matching this to "direction". Stepping back is actually instrumental in moving forward.

Expectations and Student Wait Lists

If you choose to start a Minecraft club, you may be in for a surprise. Another common story thread across teachers was that they did not quite expect the enthusiastic response that they got. Quickly, students would promote, recruit, and fill capacity in Minecraft clubs. Here are a few of these story snippets:

"I was originally thinking it would be kind of a club kind of thing. An optional activity that I'd get some kids who are already huge video game fans that would join in after school... I've had, just this year, about 150 students from our middle school playing. That is about 1/2 our middle school population."

"I invite eighth grade students into my lab during their recess time… 15 students a day because I only have about 15-16 computers. We switch off on a weekly basis. I actually have to make a list that we rotate through because I couldn't allow everyone who wanted to come in to come in."

These stories convey a sense of pride that students are showing up, but also serve as a kind of quantitative validation for the tool itself. Teachers point out that half of their students are playing because it is an expression of the relevance of the media, the broad appeal it has, and combined with previous validation elements, they are further convinced that this can serve to engage learners.

Individual students with special needs may also be part of these spaces and benefit from them. One story explained how Minecraft became a sort of intervention strategy for a student.

"The teacher approached me and said could the student please be in your Minecraft club because he doesn't care about anything else except for Minecraft and he got to the point where we did some related assignments with Minecraft and he'd actually ask to stay in at recess so he could finish it."

If you plan on trying out Minecraft outside of the classroom, plan on a crowd. If you do not want a crowd, think ahead about how you might filter or manage access to your club.

Settings, Constraints, and Goals

The overwhelming approach to after school clubs was to allow students to play as they saw fit. For all the reasons in Chapter 2, Minecraft offers plenty to players all by itself. Open play also facilitates much of the learning explained above. Stepping back, is therefore the most common approach among our participants, however we did have teachers that explained a more organized experience outside of class. Sometimes this was a follow up to open play, and other times they started out with more structure to guide students toward the kinds of things they wanted to do in the classroom later.

First, and very simply, one teacher explained that he wanted to see how Minecraft could be used for student design and exposition of their ideas. He wanted to be able to give players some constraints, (the 'box' in sandbox), and let them create within those borders.

"I put them in creative mode in the same world, the same map on creative world. I'm going to partner them up or triple them up and they are going to build essentially their dream house. A house they would be proud to show their parents. That is what we did."

In another interview, a teacher explained that a little structure was a reaction to student distractions. His players were a little younger and took on projects to build. In-game, monsters were distracting his students and frustrating their efforts.

> "I did change things. I mean that was the beginning of Minecraft in that early state. You could pick and choose features of the game to add and subtract... I also wanted to minimize distractions in the game... What I did was that I made it so that players couldn't die. They could not be hurt or killed in the game. I turned off monsters."

This minor change freed up his players to enjoy their projects and effectively engage with Minecraft. This approach requires some knowledge in how to set the play mode, how to setup the server. The teacher also put students into groups, which is fairly uncommon in this study. When asked why, the teacher explained that they had a limited number of available computers and trying out the groups would further help him to understand what Minecraft might later look like in classes. So the teacher was watching their group behaviors in addition to how they designed.

Another group of teachers built an external set of awards, badges, and community building tasks in front of their players (over 500 of them):

> "We layered over the game and the kids helped design some of those challenges. As in a normal game structure they get progressively more complex and require more collaboration as you go farther in that structure of badges so you can do lots of small things individually when you first join as a spore but then, as you level up, you are required to do more collaboration and much more complex tasks and more use of building complexity in the space."

Before you panic, this was designed by a team of teachers with the intent of inviting students from all over Australia. Their uncommon structure still allowed students to play as they saw fit, but acknowledged and communicated activities that were valued by the community, like helping a new player, learning new things, and building impressive projects. Individual teachers that used badges could do so with simply 'blocks' within the game:

> Yeah, it's something that I've developed more recently in the past couple of months. Badges. So as they walk around this world they find info blocks and it's a blue block with a white letter "i" on it. Underneath on a post is a piece of paper and if they click on that they get information.

Or 'rules' can be added outside of the game. The teacher often would challenge players to only play with certain tools, on certain settings, or gave them a narrative framework to play within. Teachers that liked to build at home could set up elaborate challenges.

"[I] decided that I needed to give them some structure so I made my very first purpose filled Minecraft world which was, the first thing I did was create a border... I put a castle up on the hill for them too. It was a puzzle how to get inside."

Naturally, teachers also reported that players would do this themselves or request a certain server setting for a session of Minecraft. Player styles often led to preferences and multiple servers being set up as the clubs refined over time. Some players enjoyed building and wanted monsters shut off and others wanted them on for survival and exploration.

Moving Toward Classroom Use

In all of these cases, the constraints and goals were more to enhance the experience than to monitor or 'manage' youth. Later, I'll talk more about social contracts, and how Minecraft provides a context for student behavior coaching and guidance. For now, it is worth noting that discipline is not present in the narrative accounts. Students are painted as enthusiastic, anxious to be in the good graces of the club advisor, and wanting terribly to see Minecraft be used in classroom settings.

"Then from there, the word sort of spread like wildfire throughout the whole school and everyone was asking about it so I began to incorporate it into some of the other classes."

Across cases, the teachers themselves tell their stories outside of class as context for how they saw potential in the classroom. Fulfilling the goals of learning the game, watching students, gaining technical skill, and sorting out group organization outside of class, some teachers began to use the clubs to experiment with curricular implementations prior to attempts in the classrooms.

One saw the differences in student play styles (from above) as an opportunity:

"I was trying to tie it into the elections this year in terms of because we have all these girls on the server and they all want to do different things. Some of them want monsters and some of them don't monsters and we have three servers because of that."

Where some may see a conflict, this teacher saw a real world opportunity to engage passionate players in a democratic resolution. This is worth unpacking a bit. Instead of teaching 'democracy' from a text, and taking a test, Minecraft cultivated an actual difference to arise between 'citizens' of a kind of digital 'country'.

When I was in the classroom, I encouraged students to visit a real city hall meeting because I wanted them to see how a city is run. Yet, even a visit to a city hall meeting may not engage student learners that do not necessarily have strong feelings about, say, where the new stop sign should be located. Students often returned to class saying it was, "Okay, but they were mostly talking about 'stuff'". That stuff was interesting to adults, (like new levies, water quality, traffic issues), but we forget how abstracted these issues are to youth—they do not yet own a home, pay bills, or drive. But In Minecraft, they do invest their own energy, time, and efforts to building a world, with other people, and they are immediately influenced by 'rule' changes the group wants to agree on. Further, students often have strong, strong opinions about them. To the teacher above, this wasn't a problem, it was the link he was looking for - real feelings, around real civic decisions, in a virtual world. We will cover a whole list of these kinds of ideas in the following chapter.

A second key story that supported moving toward the classroom included the student representation of knowledge. As students in the school become familiar with Minecraft and what things can be done within the 'blank slate' space, they often offer up alternative ways to present their work to teachers around the school. This is truly a bottom up process of technology adoption in schools.

> "The 5th grade is planning to use Minecraft because every year they build
> ziggurats out of cardboard and glue and stuff. Now they have the option to build
> the ziggurats in Minecraft."

This afterschool club is able to influence a formal classroom because the students themselves approach the teacher and ask them if they could have permission to build the ziggurats digitally instead of physically. Student choice in learning, within subject parameters, creates a powerful intrinsic tie to the work and outcomes of the class. Because the media is not essential to the experience the teacher is assigning, the swap out seems to be natural, exciting, and supporting of student interests. The same teacher points out the school wide effect of this one class adoption:

> "We are slowly working it into the school and finding ways to do things in
> different classes."

You may not start a club because you are trying to send out student advocates, yet when they get excited about their work this will likely happen.

Finally, for a few of our teachers, outside of classroom time with Minecraft *is* actually the goal. They advocate that this open time complements the highly structured classroom time during the school day. Informal learning provides an essential opportunity for youth to develop ideas, design, socialize, and connect with digital skills.

In the following chapter, we will take a look at narratives that integrate Minecraft into the classroom itself.

Starting Your First Minecraft Club

The remainder of this chapter is largely the gift of one amazing Illinois teacher and co-host of EdGamer, Zack Gilbert. I asked and he obliged to share his experience and suggestions for building a club of your own. His club ran after school, however, his guidance serves any informal youth time before school, on lunch breaks, or for a summer program. This chapter winds down then with practical guidance on starting your own club.

Zack validated the club effort, first, via his personal hobbies and conversations with a colleague.

> I always wanted to bring games to my students… Students knowing my love
> of games have asked me for years to start a club. What really pushed me to bring
> a gaming club to my school was my [friend]. He had started his game club early
> in the 2012-13 school year and he was putting a lot of pressure on me to get
> started. Gerry's success within his high school finally convinced me to get
> my club started.

Getting started means organizing who, what, where, when, establishing a 'why', and agreeing with students on how your club will be run.

Who to Involve?

Planning your club is essential. With this in mind, being aware that you are never operating alone is important. Those outside and within school should be involved in the discussion. Make a list of those that need to be considered stakeholders in your club and start having those conversations. In order, talk to the following people to get a feel for how your club might shape up:

- *Your Family.* Start involving those loved ones close to you. Will the club be taking time away from them? Are they supportive of your club idea? Can they help or be involved? If you are already a workaholic, the investment in a Minecraft club may be an idea better shared with another teacher.

- *Administration and IT Support.* Talk to Administration before talking to students. Exciting students before getting approval can lead to awkwardness and disappointment. Talking with administration early on allows them to help shape the club as part of the overall development of goals, suggest ideas to you, and address any concerns they may have. Their support is essential and will help with each following step. Depending on your administrators, you may get wholehearted support or you may need to slow down and do some persuading over time. Your IT support will have much to say if you are using digital applications or school computers in the club - make sure they are excited or at least willing to support you as needed.

- *Students.* Start with those students that you know already play Minecraft and run the idea past them. Do you have a core group of students? Are they willing to take on leadership roles? Promote? Clean? Organize events? Student enthusiasm will help to get things started, but it also will help you sustain the program over time. If they can serve to manage and lead, then it is much easier to bring in substitute supervisors if you need a day away. Zack noted he was selective in starting with a small group of students first, and building from there.

- *Fellow Teachers.* Your colleagues will be those subs. Before starting the club, take some time and check in with other teachers in your building to see if they have any interest, would be willing to help out on occasion, or if they have ideas for the club. Other teachers can help to promote the club and/or provide challenges that could tie into classroom lessons.

- *Parents.* Finally, it's time to visit your local Parent Teacher Association, send a note home to parents, or chat with them during parent-teacher conferences. You can possibly check with parents to see if you have any other adult volunteers, if they might be willing to donate or bring gaming devices (especially if your school is in short supply), or if they may be willing to financially support the club.

What should Your Club be About?

Minecraft can easily support a club, however you may want to broaden your focus to be a gaming club, game making club, or include board games or developer tools. A club can serve to challenge youth to move from high interest applications like Minecraft, or World of Warcraft, to tools that add to their gaming experience. Later we have a chapter about modifying Minecraft, but mods are common to digital gaming now. You can also show students free developer tools like Blender (3D objects), Unity (3D world building), or Scratch (entry level game logic) that can also support learner interest in a club setting.

When you choose what you are going to be doing these will lead to key planning questions.

- *Board and Tabletop Gaming.* Do you have enough space and tables? Do you have extra chairs to enable students to sidle up to game spaces? What games do you currently have? Which are your students wanting to play? Are your games appropriate for the challenge and complexity levels of your students? Do you have key players that can teach others?

- *Digital Games.* Do you have access to school computers? Do you have storage space for students to bring laptops and safely keep them until club time? Can students log into the school network? Do you need parent waivers for student play and access? Will IT need to pre-load the games or set up accounts? In the case of Minecraft, many of our teachers had IT do most of the set up (either Local Area Network or an open server) in a school lab setting.

- *Digital Production.* Moving from games to production often means upping the requirements for your processors and memory space. Will students save work on thumb drives, in the cloud, on computers, or on a server? Always check the software requirements with your school computers, or ask your IT support to check if the computers are current enough to run the software.

- *Physical Production.* Closely tied to the game design and coding communities are the maker communities. If you feel you might want to move in that direction, consider your proximity to appropriate shops, the outdoors, kitchens, janitorial support, and tools. How flexible is the space, furniture, and storage space? Do you have open floor space? Finally, you may want to double check each activity with maintenance and administration prior to starting.

Where Should You Meet?

Many teachers meet in their classrooms so they can move between desk work and being with students smoothly. However, not all teachers have computers in their classrooms to support a gaming club. Check what you are planning, and who is bringing devices, and make sure you have the right space for it. Zack also recommends a few 'comfy' chairs, couches, and open floor space to allow for diverse activities. If the right space means moving to a computer lab, cafeteria, the school library, or off site, you will need to include more people in the loop and start those conversations too. Also check the space for practical needs:

- Table spaces - with room to grow.
- Chairs - a variety for different kinds of activities.
- Outlets, extension cords, and/or surge protectors.
- Display projector/s - for group conversations and display of accomplishments.
- Online connection - WiFi saves you a lot of connectivity setup, but is a bit slower than cable/corded connections. Both will work for Minecraft.

Also think about variable conditions for the space:

- Lighting - Check that the room lighting is appropriate for computer use, reading, and design work.

- Snacks - Will you have snacks? Are vending machines in the building? Can students eat or drink in this room? What rules will you put in place?

- Garbage - Regardless of snack rules, your design work will fill a garbage can quickly. How accessible is the garbage to students? How far do they need to walk to throw something away?

- Supplies - Does the room have blank paper, graph paper, pens, markers, white boards, and other supplies for doing prototype design work? If a learner has an idea, can they get it on paper quickly and share it? Do they have access to tape or staples to hang flyers? Do you need a budget? If so, seek out parents, community organizations, businesses, or internal funding for supplies.

- Work space - If you are in another space, do you still have a place you can settle in and work when needed? Space to meet with kids away from the group? Space for small groups to plot, plan, or design together?

When Should You Meet?

Zack took considerable time sharing how important this question is.

> Your time as a teacher is important and you need to evaluate what you can handle. This will be time away from other responsibilities you have with school and your family. I believe the time I give is very important and it also helps that I thoroughly enjoy the time I spend at game club.

Carefully consider morning, lunch, after-school, summer, or even weekend times in conversation with colleagues and family. Zack used occasional Saturday 'events' for larger competitions or presentation times that parents could be more easily involved in and regularly settled into every other Friday after-school from 3:00-4:45.

Attempt to avoid conflicts. For Zack, Fridays were not a school night, so this allowed for occasionally hosting longer game nights. Consider regular community organization times, like girl scout nights, church confirmation meetings, and others. Do you need to work around these? Ask your students to check for these kinds of conflicts too. Also, check the school calendar and make every effort to avoid conflicts with other groups and events.

Set a cap on the time and communicate it up front with students. If they are unable to respect that time and get you out the door (after logging out, cleaning up, and helping to pack up) then make it clear that the club will be short lived. Sustainability is tied to your time. Part of getting you home on time is making sure that parents know the pickup time or that your group ends in time for the activity bus - especially in the middle school where students can get stranded and you are responsible to stay with them.

Make sure you communicate when the club meets effectively. Use school announcements, flyers, posters, and classroom reminders. Many of the clubs have a game club website with a calendar of events and other community assets. One group used this web site to share badges and leaderboards in the club. Also, plan to gather and use phone numbers, digital email groups, listservs, or instant messaging to communicate with parents and players when needed.

Communicating a 'Why' and Establishing a 'How'?

The front end of this chapter is primarily about why eleven of our Minecraft teachers used time outside of class to explore Minecraft. When you start a club, Zack suggests that these reasons should be clearly and consistently communicated to everyone involved. Common understanding of why you are meeting together helps to establish common goals, choose activities, and head off potential problems.

Zack started with an outline for the first students meeting to establish why they were there and how it would be run.

> "Meeting with the group for the first time was very exciting. These kids want to be here and they are coming after school to work. I don't think they realized how hard it would be to create a club, but that did not stop them. I tried to stay out of the discussion as much as possible. I wanted the students to work through the process. I did give them the outline below and told them that they can't work on any other steps until they figured out their goals for the game club."

Here is his 'first meeting' agenda for the students:

- Mission statement (Focus and goals)
- Student expectations
- What games and platforms
- Time
- Advertise and announcements
- Sponsorship and assistance

Students worked through the agenda and together agreed on their mission statement to, "Enhance learning, have fun, create, and socialize." As the core group agreed, they were establishing a culture that could be clearly communicated with other future members. They also contracted a code of behavior:

Zack's Club's Behavior Code

- Respect, Responsible, Safe
- Attendance
    - Communicate to inform the teacher you are attending
    - Parents pick up on time
- Clean up
    - Put away games appropriately with all pieces
    - Account for all pieces and inform the teacher if there is a problem

In essence, this process allowed Zack to build and communicate why they were meeting and work out how they would move forward - establishing a positive culture for the club. When there they were questions or when students had new ideas, they knew to frame them within the club goals.

Zack also assumed that his students would lead. We had a variety of teachers in the study in this regard with different attitudes about student leadership capacity. Part of why Zack is a good example of organizing a club is that by leveraging student work and input, he effectively makes the club sustainable for himself. His students figured out advertising, communications, permission slip gathering, sought out sponsors, and recruited volunteers for larger events. Students not only get the benefits of gaming in this approach, but they learn to create, organize, and work for a community group - otherwise known as civic engagement and leadership.

Meeting Times

Zack had a basic outline for how the time would be organized at the club. A few of the Minecraft teachers resisted this approach and argued for open play time. They would say that the more time the teacher structures, there is a direct loss to valuable generative time for players. Both kinds of teachers would vouch for the success of their programs.

In Zack's case we get a closer look at how time can be organized:

Basic Outline for a Game Club

- Start up (5 min):
    - Attendance.
    - All book bags and coats are left in their locker. All they need to bring is themselves. There will be time to go to lockers after club.

- They can bring any or all of the following: Laptop, tabletop game, pre-approved digital games, hand-held devices.

- Large group discussion (10 min):
  - Share new games brought and who will teach them (pick locations for each).
  - Encourage students to try something new each time they attend. If you normally play tabletop games then try a digital game. If you mainly play digital games then try a tabletop. Most students choose digital games, but are surprised at how much fun they have playing a tabletop game.

- Choose which game we will play and move to a gaming spot (2 min):
  - All students have a laptop and that makes it easier and does not force us to a lab, but we expect them to settle into a location for the time.

- Gaming time (90 min):
  - Once things get going the club is very simple to manage. The students are always engaged. You will have to monitor and make sure students are able to smoothly move from one game to another. Most will play one or two games.
  - If I get a chance, I play along with the students. I show them a new game or they can teach me a new game. We all learn best when we teach each other and this happens to many students at each game club. The students become the teachers.
  - Look for chances to lead players to higher end challenges, more complex games, and looking up ideas found in the games. Have them write and share strategies, make machinima (video re-creations), and/or research game ideas online.
  - Look for chances to lead players to design tools. Fascination with gaming often provides ideas for making their own games. When you hear, "It would be cool if…", be ready to move on that! They can make 'cool', right now. Gradually become familiar with Scratch, Game Makers, Unity, Blender, Photoshop, Illustrator, and other design tools.

- Wrap up (20 min):
  - Give a clear 20 minute warning before you expect players to log out or pack up. Games generally are designed for 15-30 minutes of action between reposes. If you 'unplug' suddenly, you can lose significant progress, planning, and even let down fellow players online (which hurts their very real reputations by being rude). Let them know that you know this rhythm of game play and that you expect that they can find a 'checkpoint' roughly every 20 minutes in a game.

- After 20 minutes, students should have started cleaning up, logging out, and generally 'leaving the space better than they found it'. If you are in your classroom, they can say 'thank you', by cleaning whiteboard, running errands, and generally helping manage the space with you.

- Those still on the computer , after 20 minutes get a 1 minute warning. After 1 minute, you can fairly power them down. Do not let fellow students do this because this is essentially a discipline situation. Talk with the student privately about the group norms and ask them to make an effort to abide by them.

- If everyone has successfully logged out without the 1 minute reminder, consider praising or rewarding this to reinforce the logout expectations. Take time to discuss the games. What did they figure out? Any good puzzles or achievements happen? Do they play or plan to play it at home? What are they going to work on next time?

- Make sure students have rides and get home on time!

Again, Zack's plan is not the only one, but it should serve to get you started, help you avoid some common pitfalls, and guide your planning a bit. If the club is organized and run well, you should get some time to play too. Try out new gaming media, challenge the students to bring you games that might work in your classroom, and shamelessly recruit students to give you lessons.

Finally, note that these clubs were often a form of validation, but they were also serving as appropriation for classes. Outside the class, you can watch students for new ideas, for natural ways to enjoy the software, and seek out student ideas as they play. After watching, listening, and building with students, teachers eventually saw an opening for their classroom ideas.

CHAPTER 7

HOW DO TEACHERS USE MINECRAFT INSIDE THE CLASSROOM?

"It's my personal opinion that an hour and ten minutes of straight typing practice is just cruel and unusual so I was trying to kind of think of something interesting that we could do other than just typing."

- Minecraft Teacher

Steal this Chapter

This chapter is primarily a summary of what these teachers did with Minecraft in their classrooms. Early in my teaching, I heard the adage, "Good teachers plan lessons, great teachers steal them," and took it to heart. Looking for 'great' ideas, I committed one prep hour per week to visit other teachers classrooms of all subject areas to see how they start class, how they organize their planning, how they led their classes. At times, I came across ideas I could copy or adopt, mostly I just enjoyed the brilliance and diversity of my colleagues. Hopefully, this chapter provides a similar experience for you and expands your list of ideas you can steal.

Everything in this book so far has led up to classroom applications. How do teachers actually use Minecraft in the classroom? How do they refine their ideas? Finally, what can we learn and what ideas can you generate when reading about what other teachers have done? Here we can start to see both common uses and a range of uses across the teacher stories. The first half of the chapter, I will present three different pedagogical approaches found across our narratives - open creative building, playing out a story, and using Minecraft to build examples and demonstrations of ideas. In the second half of the chapter, you will find classroom examples gathered around core subject areas. All of the teachers involved in this study would be flattered and excited to hear that you stole any of them for your learners - so steal, or more gently liberate, these ideas!

Creating Amazing

Like teachers using Minecraft outside of class, it is clear that first attempts to use Minecraft in the classroom were often perceived as trials under careful observation by teachers. As innovators, they are looking to see how and what learners would design with the tool before intrusively conquering it for their objectives. To do this they either use extra class time and have kids play freely, or, more commonly, start with "a basic idea" and see what they do. First the 'sandbox' examples:

> "The kids created projects on their own and worked together so at that point it didn't need to have any set curricular goals. We were just exploring."

> "It ended up being a class completely on its own with a free range of what direction we wanted to take. We ended up sort of like a sandbox class."

At this point the teachers would say they are just trying it out, seeing how the students would use it, or trying to discover new ideas. This may sound fairly chaotic in the classroom, but when pressed, these teachers also shared how they introduced students first:

> "With all four of those classes, I created a separate 'natural' Minecraft world for each one and I spent maybe 10-15 minutes at the front of the class with the kids on the floor and I was projecting on an [interactive whiteboard] and I just showed them the basics of how to move around, how to collect blocks and how to place blocks and that is really it."

So even in free play settings, teachers commonly provided introductory instruction or used game-like badges or challenges to direct early learning curves.

> "[We] developed challenges and rewards and we have upwards of 80 of those where a kid could choose a reward and then do it earning badges and leveling up."

Two important side notes: First, notice that these sample passages are very similar to teachers that had open play time in the after-school programs. This testing approach serves the teacher's learning across times. I suggest teachers that feel license to experiment in class do, and those that feel they have to convince administration more use outside of class experiences to show validity to others.

Second, for these teachers, the importance of open creative time had to be relevant to their overall classroom goals. We do not find any math or science teachers, for instance, that allowed open Minecraft time; on the other hand 'writing' teachers commonly saw the open time as generative for later writing projects. With only seventeen teachers, this is far from conclusive, but we do see hints that curricular obligations may affect pedagogical 'fit' for the teacher.

Part of 'watching' was for teachers to join in with students. They used class time for their own learning, often combining physical classroom management with online management.

> "I've always got my character on and my character is online and is in the server and sometimes I can do special things like we have restricted their water bucket usage for flooding purposes... But, yeah, I'll play with them."

Playing with students also led to collaborative design of ongoing learning for a few teachers. More teachers found that open play did not naturally lead to their learning goals.

> "Some built the Eiffel tower and others started messing around with lava. It wasn't a very constructive, cohesive production... I had imagined that some of them would get together and pioneered a little village or made something that made sense but I think the narrative that I presented them with wasn't immersive enough and didn't actually capture their imagination..."

These teachers started to experiment with more structure in the form of narratives around which the class would play a role.

Playing out a Story

A second pedagogical strategy was to have students play out a story. In these cases, teachers will share the context of game time and ask students to role play accordingly. This following example continues from where the last left off; the teacher changes what they do to add in-game and out of game elements:

> "...this time we had a project where we wanted to create an infrastructure on the island and I did some preparation where I, in cooperation with the students, mapped out different zones on the island where I said ok, we're going to have a little town here, we're going to have your private houses here and we're going to have your hotel here like your Holiday Inn kind of feel and there was a railroad going throughout the island so it was like a collaborative project where the students could help each other and also build something of their own."

While this teacher still defined their approach as "open play", they have effectively told students where to build, what kinds of things to build, and began to shape how they would interact with each other. This is not the kind of free and open Minecraft experience fostered above. This is the roughest example of the teacher shaping a story for the students to play out. In this case, it was to build a town. Students were essentially in the role of villagers and they had a job to do.

Fitting with the game itself, another common starting point is to have the students survive together. This too is a basic story, 'You are stranded on an island… what do you do?' Students are in the role of survivalist and can compete or work together to get by.

> "I had a basic idea about a group of kids being stranded on an island, inspired by the book Lord of the Flies and I said well there is a disagreement and one part of the group goes to one end [of the island] and one part of the group goes to the other end and take it from there. I just said what are you going to do? What are you going to do? They just set off building. That was basically the story."

Interestingly, some teachers chose stories with clear conflict. Lord of the Flies is a story that has youth eventually doing barbaric things to each other. These kinds of stories fit the gameplay itself and require little to no prior set up for class. Boot up the game and let them play out the story.

> "I don't want to mess with the magic too much. The further I move my lessons away from the vanilla Minecraft experience, the further I'm getting away from something that millions of gamers know and love - which is dangerous."

Outside of this study, I also talked to one teacher that had students build their world freely, get to know the game, and come to value harder to get resources in game. Yet the students were limited to their continent. To teach European exploration, the teacher then 'unlocked' the oceans and allowed players to build boats. When they reached new land they found automated non-player characters in villages. The result was that students pillaged the villages… ruthlessly… for hard to find materials. The student story played out in a way that made European-Native American interactions much more of a personal conversation for students. When the teacher connected real history to their Minecraft story, they shared one of the most powerful classroom conversations they had that year. Here the purpose of a story framework for Minecraft is to fuel experiences that the teacher can leverage for learning.

Another form of playing a story, with a bit of set up time, is to challenge students with the teacher as the antagonist! The teacher, with control of the server, has powers the players need to overcome or solve.

> "Instead of a community, they worked as a team to escape my confines. [laughter]"

> "I made a puzzle for them to get into the pyramid and I made sort of a treasure room inside. I structured it… [for the] next group of classes, the tutorial world ended up being the entirety of their Minecraft experience so they stayed on my path and with my guidance the whole time."

Most teachers played with this idea of creating an obstacle course, a first person tutorial, or setting up student play time with a constructed story as one of their early efforts. Again, this requires the teacher to make time to build and design outside of class so that the time in class is spent exploring the teacher's work. This can be done as a story outside of the game, or for some teachers, it can depart from a story and start to take the form of show and tell.

Show and Tell

Another approach to using Minecraft is to stack blocks to show an idea to others. Above, teachers gave a narrative prompt, but other teachers started experimenting with Minecraft in the classroom by challenging students to build something that was relevant to their curriculum, or curriculums:

> "It happens that we were working on our Greece unit as part of our world studies and in math we were working on rates and ratios so I thought why don't we do a little research on these and recreate some buildings."

And recreate they did. This early effort required less investment of prep time, but this initial classroom project grew, and grew and grew into what is known today as World of Humanities. World of Humanities, designed by Eric Walker, has grown into one of the most popular worlds for teachers to download. It includes most ancient civilizations and allows students to 'walk around' notable landmarks from each society. Downloading a world allows you to take advantage of impressive amounts of work, without having to build the pyramid yourself.

> "They can't build or destroy anywhere except in designated places. They start out in a tutorial area tree house and then there are info blocks that they click and then texts come up. That is the basics of it. They go around and they find the ancient China area and they explore and they learn about all the things we've talked about in class, about ancient China or ancient Greece or the islands of mythology or the pyramids. There are tons of areas now. I've been adding to it constantly and students have too. There are specific areas where students can build and those are, there are some housing areas which are more popular at first… there is an area where they can build different schools in different styles of either Athens or Sparta, and they have to match their educational philosophies which is something we learn about in class. There is an area where they can learn how to build defense systems for an ancient city, Babylon in this case. They create an irrigation system to show how irrigation, how the Mesopotamians brought water from the Tigris and Euphrates Rivers and then created farming and agriculture. There is an area where they are just a landscape architect and are building gardens around the Lighthouse of Alexandria and a ton more than that."

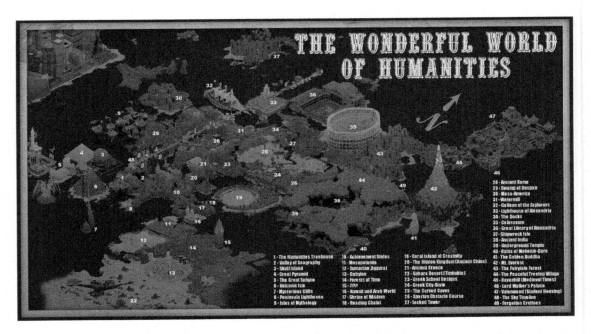

Image 1: Eric Walker's *World of Humanities*. Source: http://dig.temple.edu/wp-content/uploads/2013/03/World-of-Humanities-Map-Feb-20131.jpg

Walker designates areas for seeing, areas for particular tasks, and areas for student building. This mix allows for different play styles, but also allows the teacher to nudge players in different directions within a complex learning environment. He sees these worlds as a giant classroom space for students to explore and learn from. This approach allows for Minecraft to operate as a presentation tool also. Another teacher used Minecraft for short demo's in the classroom:

> "I was teaching a group of... 15 year olds about neurotransmitters and redstone is perfect for how neurotransmitters work so I set up a little room and a little demonstration of what neurotransmitters do and how they have to cross the synapses... so it was just a small trial, [15-20 minutes], with a class of say 17 students, just one short activity, minimum amount of set up time and it was just amazing."

This, of course, could be seen as a unique form of teasing; putting one of the most popular video games up on the big screen. Later this teacher allowed students to role play cells and he set them on fire (inside the game). As they attempted to run, he explained that when heated up, cells do the same thing - combining a show and tell setting with a kind of science 'story' experience. Naturally, the follow up assignment is to invite students to represent what they know by building their own Minecraft 'labs', showing or using short video demos, and/or actually printing physical versions of their creations.

"Now I'm moving into the 3d printing world so using it as a 3d modeling tool so students can create models using Minecraft."

Minecraft classrooms use strategies that seem to include either creative building, playing out a story, or using Minecraft to model concepts. In fact, many of our teachers played with more than one pedagogical approach without any clear progression from one to another. Teachers that started with open creative building time, would often add story their next try. Conversely, teachers that had highly guided demonstrations, continued by allowing students open build time. That said, if you are looking for a 'best practice' for Minecraft, this data suggests that all three are part of understanding the tool and its uses. You'll see below that subject area ideas for Minecraft employ these strategies in creative ways.

Using Minecraft within Subject Areas

When you choose to try Minecraft in the classroom, you may have a particular subject you are responsible for in mind. This chapter contains a variety of classroom uses and examples of teachers using Minecraft across subject areas. One goal is to have a quick reference, however I would encourage you to read examples from outside your subject area too. Many of these teachers saw ideas from other teachers and modified them to fit. If you want a particular idea, this is far from an exhaustive list of ideas and teachers suggested visiting online sites, like Minecraft EDU, for connecting with and sharing ideas with other teachers. Here, however, you can get a good sense and feel for how the above approaches are applied in classroom settings.

First, once you have played Minecraft a bit, you may see that some of the natural activity in the game already serves your curriculum. You can explore this deliberately, as one of our teachers did:

> "I took out all the essential standards, all the ones that lended themselves very well to the whole Minecraft interface… So, we have been talking about forces of motion with the roller coaster aspect of Minecraft and talking about digging speeds and velocities and things like that…"

I would add that this can be done *with* students too. Sharing your entire course 'calendar on the wall' (or COW)[1] introduces the goals of the class and involves students in the common challenge of classroom work. Having students share ideas is not only effective professional learning for teachers, it is also engaging and fosters ownership of the learning process.

---

[1] I'm really not sure on the actual source for 'COW'. This is an idea my principal, Tom Harrold, shared with my middle school team of teachers a decade or so ago. We mapped the curriculum in order to find existing interdisciplinary opportunities.

COW can be used in any subject that has clear curricular goals, and many ideas for classroom use arose because teachers knew their goals and were able to see connections. Art, technology, architecture, and exploratory teachers more often approached Minecraft as an open sandbox. Across our teachers, we saw subject specific applications arise in the core subject areas: science, math, writing, and social studies. I'll attempt to show breath of application in the following examples.

Science Stories

Use of Minecraft as a lab is suggested above. More ideas supported this approach in teacher narratives. For example:

> "So what we did is rocks and minerals and I asked one of my Minecraft players to make a video which he did an amazing job of an overview of all the different types of rocks and minerals in Minecraft."
>
> or
>
> "I built a massive cell model they can walk through with students creating plant cells."

Really, anything physical can be 'built' in Minecraft. Students could build a cell, human heart, or a digestive system, in biology; or landforms, water bodies, and minerals for geology. In each of these examples, Minecraft is used as a 'lab' lesson, where the teacher introduces the activity and then supports it during the classtime:

> "I was more of the person on the side, you know, the lead scientist, so I didn't have to do anything, I just had to supervise them. I've walked them through it and given them specific activities like the neurotransmitters maps or an open exploration with the cell map."

Image 2: A Minecraft Digestive System Science Project. Source: http://www.reddit.com/r/Minecraftcomments/ 1gdxmt/my_extra_credit_project_for_biology/ and too_many_toasters

Minecraft, like typing paper, can be used to represent ideas effectively and in a 3D space that is exciting.

Minecraft can be used as a context for scientific thinking too. One teacher looked beyond the 'building' nature of Minecraft, and saw that Minecraft essentially encouraged a kind of planning and purposeful thinking. He used this planning as a pathway into scientific thinking.

> "So he would sit down and write 'the next time I play Minecraft I want to find out' and so from that he did science and then I said lets do predictions so from around that we did the science of inquiry. What are your theories? What are your predictions? That is how we scaffolded learning so that is what I mean when I say we take that interest and then I build on it and we go and we did."

Elements within the game can also be a focus of investigation. When students conduct more advanced crafting, or you turn on creative mode, they will find TNT in game. TNT explodes according to formulas already programmed into the game. Likewise, when you drop from a height, your character takes different amounts of damage based on the height of the fall. Day and night seem regular and the sun seems to 'move', so how is time linked to real time? How might a scientist explore these 'natural' phenomena? How long do different materials take to burn? How have scientists historically taken hypothesis toward law with data collection, replication, and measuring predictive algorithms?

As with science in the natural world, Minecraft provides a virtual world that can be explored, studied, and serve as a giant lab for the scientific process.

Writing & Language Arts

An obvious starting point is to have students re-create things they read:

> "I've seen students create book reviews so they are creating a scene from a book and then walk through it and talk about a book they've read."

Some of the more interesting story ideas create a context for players to experience a story, and then write. I remember my own writing teacher saying, 'Most great writing is reflecting, in part, on the writers own journeys." Yet if students are still inexperienced and overly curated, they may not have much to write about[2]. For instance, Hemingway went to war and did some Caribbean fishing before he sat down to write - yet neither are available for most of our students. In digital games, however, students can experience great adventures, save the world, or play out very real dramas with fellow players. For these lessons, the teacher can easily have students play the story.

> "We went at it from stranded on a desert island perspective. They get in the world. They are doing survival mode so its up to them to gather their resources, to pool their talents, to find shelter, to avoid danger and they are blogging about that experience."

---

[2] Leading, arguably, toward the thin fabrications and ponderous poetry assignments many of us remember in our own writing classes; 'If only you could 'dig' deeper!!' ;)

In the absence of real danger, students can safely have play danger. Using blogs also introduces a newer format and genre to students. The point here is that the story happens to the students first, then they write from memory, not purely imagination. Immediately, this opens the curriculum up to travel journals, memoirs, blogging, archiving history, or ethnographic work in multiplayer worlds.

This kind of immediacy is engaging and consistently hooks students - even when they are trying to 'kill' each other:

> "I teach an elective class about the Hunger Games. We use the Hunger Games and we incorporate technology projects. We basically went through and recreated the setting of the story district 12 in Minecraft. It was just a great way to tie in what they were learning and what they were reading in a really fun and interactive way."

This example models existing effective teaching around a novel. Other projects have rebuilt Hogwarts, Azeroth, Middle Earth, and King's Landing. Using print media to inspire drawing, writing, conversation, or film making is established practice in language arts. In these cases, Minecraft simply adds another media format to play out what they are reading or playing.

Conversely, Minecraft design can be inspired by external resources. One teacher treated another computer game as source material and had students use Minecraft to build similar story arcs with 'quests'.

> "We had a project where we did level design with the guys and had them write a story. We were inspired from the quests from Skyrim where there was very clear progression in the quests."

For this class, students would build contexts for their story and invite friends to come and play their stories. This uses Minecraft as the composition media. Instead of pure prose, the 'writers' had to build puzzles, clues, prompts, and post signs that carried a player from beginning to the end of their adventures. Finally, I would think these had to be a pleasure to grade/play when they were turned in.

Social Studies

When I first started playing Minecraft with my own two kids, we quickly built our dream houses and looked for the next thing to build. Like Eric Walker, we started to think about existing buildings that would be fun to build and the kids helped to bake bricks for a recreation of Independence Hall in Philadelphia.

> "Through textbooks and though movies and through in-class activities, they can kind of get a glimpse of being enveloped in this other world, but it isn't really deep... I always wanted to somehow communicate to my kids that there was this whole other world that you could explore, and it's fun to do so."

This is probably the simplest entry point for social studies teachers. Have students start exploring new worlds or have them start to build things to demonstrate of what they know.

Image 3: Beginning to build a colonial village with Independence Hall. Source: Author.

"I'm going to have them create a pioneer town and if I can do it to scale I might have them do that. I'll have to find plans and stuff like that. That is the next big project after this one."

To build a pioneer town, they have to do some research. "Finding plans" is no simple task, but made much easier with the internet. These kinds of ideas can continue to be refined by using particular historic texts, for instance, to build sets for events - like building colonial Boston for Johnny Tremain, or having the class set up camp by states at Valley Forge.

Another approach is to consider Minecraft less as a modeling tool and more of a multiplayer world. One teacher set classroom rules (no 'in game' settings needed) to only use certain tools each day to represent technological development.

"The latest project right now is the CivCraft project which is Civilization and the goal is to play through stone age, iron age and bronze age and we are working from a Danish context so we'll progress through Viking time and into the Middle Ages and this has been a great experience for seeing what a teacher can do because I'm able to develop my own content."

This kind of approach allows conversation around constraints each day and helps students connect with events from personal experience. So, in terms of history classes, students can see history, build history, or play out history. None of our teachers had students act out scenes from history, but I would see this as another easy application of Minecraft.

Minecraft actually has 'biomes' that define computer generation areas in new worlds. These biomes map fairly well onto Geography classes. Using Minecraft to identify landforms, water bodies, and to introduce irrigation or cartography are all fairly easy class lessons to develop. Human-Environment interaction is the core game mechanic for Minecraft and any of those themes would be low hanging fruit. Further, students can engage together in massive terraforming projects that may work for different kinds of geographical studies.

The World of Humanities example above could, and are, being expanded to current cultural studies. Teachers and students build modern cities and communities as a way to root discussions and lessons about modern places.

Image 4: Guild construction of a Minecraft City. Source: http://imgur.com/gallery/tsiKf and highrossferry

These larger projects require teamwork too. Many of our teachers explain that Minecraft leads to conversations about working together, teamwork, civics, and respect (next chapter). These aspects of citizenship can be expected as you progress in the classroom and are on the radar especially for social studies teachers that are looking for ways to teach citizenship.

> "The next thing is this big project on digital citizenship where the sixth grade is going to create a world where everyone practices exemplary digital citizenship…"

Knowing the software and the issues of ownership and property that are tied to creating things in a common space, teachers can expect these issues to be learning opportunities. Or one teacher approached the idea far more directly and had students designing abstract representations of values:

> "I had this idea of how about if they represent our school standards, responsibility, respect, honesty, safety, cooperation, if they represent one of those ideas abstractly it would be like a sculpture... I had them make a model of it in tinfoil first so they have a common leaving off point."

Of course the tinfoil models were tabletop sized, and the Minecraft versions were more building sized.

Overall, no teacher stayed strictly within their subject area confines. Combining sculpture with social studies, science labs with scaled perfection, and mixing story inspiration with story representation are all common across the teachers we talked to. They explained consistently that Minecraft is a blank slate, a piece of paper, ready to be drawn on. So one activity generally leads to another. Building Mount Rushmore leads to a study of sculpture, laying out a road for Bilbo Baggins means pacing out a "day's walk", terraforming leads to predictive hypothesis of TNT explosions. Your role, regardless of your approach to using Minecraft in the classroom, is to frame the lens through which players will look at, design in, and compose stories within a powerfully flexible space.

Far from a complete listing of Minecraft ideas, this chapter attempted to show a range of them from within the teachers narratives to support your planning for your classrooms. For most teachers, however, planning an activity goes hand in hand with evaluating learning. Most teachers in this study were as interested in some kind of evidence of benefit to their students, as they were in the activity itself. The following chapter helps us to see what they see and what they are looking for when they use Minecraft in the classroom.

CHAPTER 8

HOW DO TEACHERS EVALUATE MINECRAFT LEARNING IN THE CLASSROOM?

"It wasn't a matter of them measuring up to our expectations, they totally exceeded them…"

- Minecraft Teacher

More than a Test

For classroom teachers, the end of the chapter has some ideas for using Minecraft as an evaluation tool. Minecraft teachers also *evaluated* Minecraft activities and the bulk of this chapter puts a spotlight on how they choose to do this. Subject area content is important to these teachers, but is not consistently or predominantly on the minds of Minecraft teachers when they evaluate classroom use of Minecraft. Instead, they gauge a lesson quite differently than we might expect. Across our interviews, Minecraft teachers assessed the value of their new lessons based on: their own learning, student engagement/motivation, social skill building, and problem solving.

At first glance, building a block house seems like it may not be related to core subject areas at all - and might possibly be a complete waste of time. Even when the ideas in the last chapter played out well, some teachers spent large amounts of prep time and class time delivering the content. Is it worth the time? Is it relevant to the curriculum? Some teachers in the study were keenly aware of this balance:

> "I have curriculum to deliver and assessment to do and recording to get done. I can not just let them play. I don't know if that is short sightedness on me or whether that is just a fact."

Teachers have a mandate to teach particular skills, subjects, and tools to their learners - they are not babysitters. As a society, we demand that teachers keep this focus and have an expectation that they actually plan for and evaluate innovative ideas, at least in part, based on their ability to teach curricular content. So, the time/learning ratio question is legitimately posed, not just to Minecraft teachers, but to any new idea for the classroom. Teachers should always be evaluating a new idea by asking, 'Is this activity adding appropriate value for the time spent?'. This chapter starts by asking exactly how Minecraft teachers evaluate new classroom practices.

Where I expected that at least a few of the teachers would brag about increased test scores, few did. Their focus was not necessarily on test prep, rote memorization, or trivia facts. Some teachers even rejected these as distractions to the larger goal of raising children. Most looked at these elements as only a part of what they were designing for in the classroom. Subject area learning came *after* other relevant signs that they were on the lookout for.

In narrative analysis this is significant.

Narratives reveal what the storyteller values and what they think the listener needs to hear. For instance, if you were to tell about a new piece of software you are using, you may show it, then talk about its speed and cost. This kind of 'story' details the artifact, but also allows us to see what you value. Namely, you justify your choice with what you perceive is most important about it or what you think will persuade the listener. In the example, you are revealing that you value software that saves you time and money. Time and money are relevant measures, or evaluators, of the software.

Likewise, when teachers share classroom ideas, they commonly provide introductions and epilogues that they perceive are relevant evaluation points of the idea itself. So, when they share that the lesson resulted in increased test scores, we can reasonably conclude they think test scores are important measures of success. With the national conversation on accountability, scores, remediation, value-added activities, and standards, we expect innovative teachers to qualify their stories with test results. Yet, test results are clearly not what these teachers valued most.

> "In many ways [these] are even more important than the active standards in which we test students on all the time."

Great lessons are about more than a test. Minecraft teachers occasionally explain how students learn content, but more often include what *they* were learning, student engagement, motivation, learned behavioral social skills, and problem solving behavior. These goals appear as they tell about Minecraft, and remain as constant measures of success in their classrooms. "Across cases, Teachercrafters share that a 'good lesson' involves these key outcomes:

- Teacher learning,
- Student motivation and engagement,
- Community building,
- Student problem solving, and
- Curricular learning.

Minecraft provided a context to measure all five of their valued outcomes. None of these should come as a surprise to an experienced educator and they are *common* evaluation elements across narratives in this study. Yet, we may often train teachers to look only for what students have memorized (curricular learning) without necessarily training them to look for and value whether or not *they* learn when they try a new idea, or if their students are learning to work together.

For Minecraft teachers, these values are not secondary to curricular learning, they are equal to, or if anything, supercede curricular learning as outcomes that matter. They focus on the software within a larger classroom experience and how it played into that experience. They go out of their way to clarify the primary importance of non-curricular evaluation of lessons:

> "Our primary goal isn't to fill them with knowledge but to create experiences from whence we can draw knowledge"

Commonly, in research, we measure an input with pre and post testing to see what content is learned, yet not one of our teachers narrated this as a validation of their use of Minecraft. It is not clear that these knowledge based measures of learning are irrelevant, but they are at least competing with other goals the teachers had, for instance:

> "I can point to academic standards and say this reaches that standard but there is no standard for managing your time or for collaborating with the person sitting next to you or for organizing a team and assigning jobs."

These Minecraft teachers want students to do more than memorize. Life and work skills are of greater importance and at the edge of the kind of thinking valued by these teachers. They suggest that students need to exercise imagination, creativity, or ingenuity around sticky problems. So, they are generally looking for evidence of student thinking, engagement and motivation, positive social behaviors, problem solving, and also curricular learning. In short, Minecraft teachers are looking for engagement more than scores, problem solving more than 'correct' answers, and evaluate the use of Minecraft based more on their own professional learning than on any external recommendation.

Learning from Students

Teachers, seeking higher level thinking habits, have to find a balance between work that is too easy and too hard for the largest number of their students. This requires years of observing students when trying new lessons and a refined expertise in reading student reactions. As we saw in Chapter 5, these Minecraft teachers are experts at watching. They sample ideas with students, test them after school, and informally seek feedback from their charges; so classroom implementation is a logical extension of these validation techniques.

When trying out an idea in the classroom, watching student reactions is the final test of a lesson idea - this is central to their ability to pursue promising lesson ideas and reject ones that come up short. Watching students in the classroom is not separate from validating an idea, it is part of the same process. Learning from students is a skill that Minecraft teachers take for granted, and therefore shows up in their stories.

Curiously, it was not always considered a bad thing when students were confused or challenged by instructional designs. Convinced Minecraft was good for her students, one teacher explained:

> "I would say most of the rest of them were overwhelmed by it. Like, 'What are we supposed to do?' 'What is the assignment?' 'Why are we here?' 'What is the goal?' 'Where do I find the treasure?' You know, stuff like that."

Typically, an overwhelmed student is bad. For this teacher it was an observable sign that the students were asking the right questions and that the activity was pushing them to think for themselves. So the 'overwhelmed' students had to start thinking differently, creating, planning, and exercising the part of their brain that had been starved in highly structured learning spaces. In this case, 'overwhelmed' was a sign that the design was effectively frustrating students that needed to increase their ability to think for themselves.

Teachers are trained to design lessons that carefully scale difficulty toward every student successfully learning. For instance, I remember having to turn in daily lessons, as a young teacher, that started with SWBAT (Students will be able to). But in practice, that outcome often is less clear and very diverse student populations can start into new content with confusion and difficulty - or mastery.

'Overwhelmed' is not bad, it is inevitable; how a teacher deals with it, however, marks that teacher quality can be learned. Notice, above, that the teacher says, "You know, stuff like that", as though this is common knowledge. To a practicing teacher, or at least to Minecraft teachers, 'overwhelmed' is simply part and parcel to testing new ideas. Their initial confusion, then, is not as relevant as what students do after starting confused. Does the lesson eventually lead to clarity? Do students help each other out? Are they motivated enough by the goal to overcome 'overwhelmed'? These are what Minecraft teachers are looking for when they try a lesson.

So, consistently, our teachers explain how they first want to watch students wrestle with Minecraft and figure it out. They were checking their own expectations against student performance. Instead of making things simpler, they first wanted to see what happened in the face of a real challenge:

> "We would have never seen what the kids would do if we had managed it with a curriculum instead of stepping back to watch where the kids would go with it.

This is interesting. This implies that the teacher has some learning to do with every lesson they try out. Teaching with Minecraft, or other digital games, requires teacher-designers to explore the medium for themselves.

Also, after narrating their story, Minecraft teachers show value by comparing problem-based learning to 'managed', or outcome-based, curriculum. What is the difference? Managed curriculum implies unified delivery of common lessons so the average student will master the content knowledge. For non-teachers, this is the bread and butter of all textbook based curricular material or even much of today's digitized curriculum. This may be good for making sure even the average student keeps up, but extremely limiting to quick learners and alienating to slow learners. Differentiation or project-based learning allows all learners to perform at their own level. The goal is that all students advance their skills, thinking, and learning - not a common standard, or 'bar', to jump over.

This is a subtle shift in thinking, but illuminating: Minecraft teachers often challenge, rather than assign; cheer and challenge, rather than provide incentives; and watch students, rather than having students watch them. As teachers they guide, but even the popular 'guide on the side' approach doesn't quite capture the degree to which they favored the term "watch" instead. 'Guide' still implies that the teacher initiates and directs learning, watch implies that teachers wait for students to some degree and then react.

Notice in chapters 6 and 7 that some teachers invested considerable time in preparing Minecraft lessons. 'Watching', in these narratives, looks more like when a filmmaker watches audience reactions to their film. It is active and framed by a set of expectations that the teacher has for the time spent. Teachers that used a more open approach would set the parameters of classroom activity and expect students to 'play' along with those. From there, these teachers were still curious, active observers of what students would do within those parameters. Like laboratory researchers setting up an experiment, these teachers honestly wanted to see what would happen and to what degree students would surprise, impress, come up short, or delight them with their work.

"It wasn't a matter of them measuring up to our expectations, they totally exceeded them…"

So when expectations are met, the evaluation of the lesson is positive. When they are not, the teacher would presumably go looking for new ideas. Minecraft teachers often explain a degree of surprise at student performance, because having all students follow the same steps, they explain a goal and watch students discover their own path toward it.

"I've found is that there is always one or two students in my class who if they aren't experts, they are pretty close and they are definitely one or two students in each of my classes who knew more than I did."

Watching, or learning from students, is standard practice among Minecraft teachers, and is consistently narrated as justification for using Minecraft in the classroom. Practically, when they watched, they were able to learn the appropriate level of challenge, allow the activity to set the pace for students, and intercede or redirect when needed. Others also watched for opportunities to teach, assign challenges, new lesson ideas, or just student delight in lesson designs and suit their own curiosity. In the stories, these are conveyed not just in terms of Minecraft use, but as a benefit to their practice in general. Particularly, they look for motivation and engagement.

Motivation and Engagement

Minecraft teachers share that student engagement is one of the ways they saw that Minecraft was working in their classrooms. Engagement is an observable sign of motivation and the two are used interchangeably by our teachers. Where other work provides more precise definitions of these terms, I will reflect the looser general use found in the narratives. Each story is supported with a comment about engagement or motivation. This one is a bit awkward, but it is representative of how the teachers connected engagement to a range of other learning benefits.

"I think this project was one of the best I've had so far because it was a high level of engagement and we're working with multiple skills… they were training at the same time."

So why is engagement important? Obviously, it is nice if students are motivated, but they can still learn even when it is just… work. Can't they? I have also heard teachers argue that it is not their job to motivate students - students should see the benefit of learning prior to setting foot in the classroom. Shouldn't they? Surely, engagement and motivation are not as valuable a measure as test scores, yet Minecraft teachers used these as internally valid justifications for using Minecraft in the classroom. Why?

"I haven't specifically used the word engagement yet, but that is the first
thing that anyone should mention. It is really powerful when you hear a kid say,
'I used to hate waking up in the morning and coming to school, but [now]
I can't wait to get there.' That's really meaningful."

First, these teachers both value engagement and assume that a motivated student eventually learns more than a non-motivated students. Where this study does not confirm or deny this link, we can see more specifically what about engagement was valuable to Minecraft teachers. Motivated students spend more time on task and universally improve learning across abilities and learning styles.

"They are motivated to become experts on the game. They do their own
research at home. They figure out their own strategies. It really takes on a life
outside the classroom walls. I think that is something that every teacher should
be trying to do."

Second, Minecraft teachers are looking for engagement as a sign they have addressed learning styles. Some of the teachers appreciate that different students learn differently, so any lesson that engages a number of different types of learners catches their attention. This teacher calls them 'player types' in relation to the game.

"I wanted to create activities for each of these player types."

These kinds of activities are rare and usually require resources and time (like field trips), so when a software application challenges *and* engages, this is worth telling me about in an interview:

"The time on task is 90-100%. I've been working with middle school for a year
and a half and what I've noticed is that just doesn't usually happen. They are the
most off track people I know but they are willing to sit at a computer and look
stuff up and when they get frustrated with things they go find resources that
will help them."

Time on task, as a measure of engagement, speaks to efficiency of classroom hours. Practicing teachers know that time is precious and they weigh activities not only on how much curricular learning is happening, but on the degree to which the activity draws learners into the material. Because, especially with younger learners, this can lead to learning outside of class, investment in engagement and motivation can lead to larger payoffs in curricular learning. Traditionally, an 'anticipatory set' has served to quickly pull students out of the hallways and into focus, but these teachers treat entire lessons as engagement tools or as supplements to the larger goals of the class. This opens up understanding evaluation not just as lesson to lesson, but unit to unit, or even course to course.

Third, engagement and motivation is observed when students are acting like professionals. Minecraft teachers want to see that their students have engaged with class content so much so that when they observe the student it looks more like they are playing at a hobby than doing their school work.

> "All my colleagues are saying [the students] aren't working together and they come into the minecraft class and they have prepared in their breaks what they are going to do and they come in and sit and are totally engaged for one and a half hours and when the lesson is over I have to tell them we are finished now you have to log off."

This is evidence, to this teacher, that a student can act differently in different classes based on the experience the teacher provides. I would suggest that the comparison is not the point here, but the notable shift in engagement is at the root of their justification. They evaluate the effectiveness of Minecraft by observing student engagement; and engagement is not bound by classroom minutes. Across stories, Minecraft teachers shared tips on how to arrange classrooms (so you can see all screens from the middle), using tools to 'finish' class (MinecraftEDU has a 'freeze' function for teachers), and students that went home to learn more about a subject because they were engaged in the subject material.

> "He had a student last year who came up to him and said, 'Sir, I have been reading about China,' and we were just about to start the unit on ancient China, 'And I know everything about it.' [The teacher] was like, sure, yeah, whatever, not really believing it but wanting to encourage his enthusiasm. As the unit started and a couple of weeks in, he would be saying something and then the student would raise his hand and say, 'Yeah, and then this is what happened.' He would basically be saying all of the factual information before the teacher could even say it. He actually did know most of the facts and information of the unit. It was all from [Minecraft]..."

The story continues with a clear connection between why engagement and motivation are important, finally, because they actually lead to content area knowledge. Prior to summative assessment of a lesson, effective Minecraft teachers use constant formative assessment of engagement and motivation because:

> "...He really took it upon himself, when he knew that ancient China was coming up, to go explore that area, read every little single info block, take little notes on it, and sure enough he knew all the basic facts and information. Now of course, he didn't understand completely from our in-class activities and our reflection papers and things like that, but so far as pre-existing knowledge, it blows away anything."

Positive Social Outcomes

Closely related to engagement and motivation, Minecraft teachers evaluated effective learning plans based on how students related socially during the implementation of the lesson/s. Students, when engaged can work together out of pure enthusiasm. This is easy when they are friends outside of class, but evidence of effective learning designs when observed between non-friends.

> "So, this little group of kids that wouldn't talk to each other outside of class unless forced are working together and figuring out or delineating their roles in the town."

> "One or two kids figured out the mechanics of farming really quickly so they were the experts and helped others. Some of the kids that were good at building would build little barns for other groups. They would specialize..."

This teacher observed students negotiating 'roles' and was impressed as much by their ability to work across social partitions as their content area learning. This speaks again to their desire to teach the whole student. Part of growing up is to learn to talk and work with those that you may not spend time with socially. This social element of evaluating a lesson is reinforced even outside of the teacher's own practice.

> "I actually had my principal come into my class to sub a couple of weeks ago during this typing class and she has not been able to stop talking about it since she came in for that very reason. She said she saw students who she has never seen open up before were actively involved and engaged and they were getting along and she has just been really interested ever since."

Student behavior was consistently reported as not a problem when using Minecraft. In fact, because most behavior infractions happened within the digital world (griefing, stealing, and/or respect issues) the teachers shared that these were abstracted a bit and made counseling the students easier.

For instance, when one kid started to dig under another student's house, the latter complained. The teacher does not tell the story as a negative aspect of Minecraft, but instead interprets this as an opportunity to talk about respect for 'space' issues that the student had outside of Minecraft. Other problems arose when outside students were allowed into the class server:

> "The most serious thing was when a student invited his cousin who didn't go to our school to play and the cousin started using swear words and all kinds of stuff like that. So, I printed out the chat log that I can get from monitoring the server, gave it to our assistant principal, it was on her desk the next day, talked to the kid who invited him, had him sit down after school."

Otherwise, negative class behaviors were perceived consistently as minimized by student engagement in Minecraft activities, class expectations, and the threat of losing the 'privilege' to work on projects in Minecraft.

> "We're finding students that are doing really well with Minecraft are having fewer discipline issues in other classes."

> "It's almost bad because I'm afraid that when I do get some negative reactions I won't have had practice in how to handle it."

Finally, Minecraft teachers noted when students started to help each other. This is especially important when setting up a project-style lesson. One teacher will have a difficult time answering every question that comes up. However, when some students that are excelling at a project can handle basic questions, the teacher will take notice and appreciate the help. A teacher that tells content might be concerned when a student 'takes over', a teacher that sets expectations is relieved. A variety of class settings allows some students to excel in a Minecraft project, where they may not in other classroom settings. This teacher points this out and shows how they see emergent leadership as relevant in evaluating a lesson.

> "It is good to see that situation where kids who are exasperating to a typical teacher, they aren't in this situation. They end up being the teachers themselves."

Overall, Minecraft teachers consistently looked for social behaviors in students. When using Minecraft they saw positive work habits, helpfulness, and students connecting with other students outside of their normal friendships. They appreciated the chance to work with students on real social issues, but use in-game situations to root the conversation. Finally, Minecraft already has a few million kids ready to be helpful, show others, and take on leadership in classrooms that use Minecraft.

Problem Solving

Problem solving could also be categorized as a form of positive social behavior. However, when looking across the Minecraft stories, teachers treated this as a unique feature. Perhaps because 'problem solving' is treated as both a social skill and as a learning goal in literature and professional conversations today (STEM initiatives, 21st Century Skills, or the Games for Learning community). Minecraft teachers agreed that the purpose of a learning design is to create a setting for problem solving.

> "We are teaching them how to think… We encounter a problem and there are things they have to deal with and sometimes they are looking at YouTube videos and doing how to's and teach each other how to do things…"

If teachers are less focused on presenting information, it follows that they have this kind of focus on teaching learners how to find information, sort it, and apply it to tasks. This is internally valuable:

> "It is great to see them problem solving because I don't think they are getting enough of that."

Minecraft teachers, at times, explained their use of Minecraft, similarly, as a kind of supplement to the kinds of cognitive activity missing elsewhere in the school day. Similarly, these teachers recognized a gap in school curriculum around learning professional editors and teaching youth programming code languages.

Learning complex software to accomplish goals, (even silly ones), is relevant evidence of some students embracing problem solving behavior because of classroom exposure to Minecraft. Minecraft teachers regularly explain that Minecraft is a "gateway drug" for professional software and/or learning to use professional digital tools. So when a student engages with Minecraft, they commonly want to know more about how to make videos, change server settings, program their own features, use graphic software to design new outfits for their character (skinning), build group calendars and web sites, organize events for other games, or look at professional editing software.

Problem solving improves as they play the game, because larger projects require teamwork and communication. This too stands out when they share the results of using Minecraft. Teachers explain that they see growth over time in problem solving skills. Effective problem solving can be larger class conversations (classroom planning meetings) or they can be smaller, efficient, communication that the teacher observes:

> "Students were just organically building and deciding as they went with very little communication; just deciding where things would go and how something would be. That's really fascinating, how much or how little communication they use when they are building together and how organic that is and how they negotiate how that will turn out."

I would suggest that these kinds of informal observations are primary evaluators among the teachers in this study, along with rubric assessment, traditional testing, and student presentations of their work.

On the other hand, in order to represent the range of teaching philosophies in this study, Minecraft does not have to evaluate anything to be valuable. Where some teachers felt an obligation to teach content, other teachers insisted that Minecraft naturally leads to many of the positive outcomes listed above. They argue that overt evaluation, (especially grades and summative assessments), can be intrusive and even reduce the benefits (like high motivation or intrinsic rewards) that a game like Minecraft already offers its players. They, along with others, advocate for the value of increasing free time, play, and hobby spaces that allow lifetime learning without expectations.

Evaluating a Minecraft Assignment

This chapter wouldn't be quite complete without sharing some of the ways that these teachers used Minecraft as a tool for students to show their work. Many of the teachers did want to see subject area learning too and asked students to show what they had learned. Minecraft projects are commonly shared with the teacher as a picture, by opening up the game and doing a 'tour' of work done in the game, by writing about experiences in Minecraft, by taking a test on the subject matter, or by creating a video using screen capture software. Most teachers had tried more than one of these approaches across iterations and even on the same project. One interesting approach was to use external software to 'pull' Minecraft projects into a virtual reality.

> "An app called Minecraft Reality... you know chunking out the segment of their space and creating it and putting it into an augmented reality thing we can set it on their [desk], view it, and... and the kid can walk around and show their creation."

After the interview I tested this out. Using an iPad as a lens, the software marks a real location as you move the camera lens around it. Then it locates the Minecraft project within that location. On a desk, the floor, or in a gymnasium for a 'fair' like event. Students can show off their Minecraft projects in a variety of ways. All of these presentation methods depend on the project itself representing or demonstrating what the student has learned.

This looks very similar to any project-based learning environment, starting with establishing clear expectations, or criteria, for the project. Some teachers told the students what these expectations were or gave them as a written assignment or rubric. One teacher worked with students to build the criteria for the project.

> "We'll find examples of product that approximates what we would like to do and say, 'What makes this good? What makes this not good and what makes something better? What qualities do you want to see in a good product?' Then those become our project criteria and so when the student is working on a project, they'll look back at the criteria and say have I met those criteria? Does my product fit the criteria for being a good or an excellent product."

This teacher continues to point that this is effective professionally and they are attempting to teach and model self-evaluation. Depending on the project, criteria may include: accuracy, scale, details added, creativity, clarity of an idea, peer evaluations, or content area questions about the project.

Final work usually had students communicating the expectations of the class within their Minecraft work. It is the learner's job to synthesize work and make the connection.

> "What I had them do there was to record themselves giving a tour through their creation and so they narrated a walk through of their environment and highlighted the things they wanted me to notice. [Learners] highlighted where they integrated concepts from social studies. Then I tell them to try to get those down to a five to seven minute video that I could watch and could assess and see their learning outcome."

This particular example includes both Minecraft and video editing software - and requires students to learn the editing software because they want to show the Minecraft work. Essentially, these teachers value 'show and tell' after 'time on task'. Showing can take on a variety of media formats and include photos, videos, written work, new programs, or a combination of these elements; telling requires that students understand and can operationalize their work within the content area; and time on task implies learner focus, engagement, and efficient use of time inside and outside of the classroom.

CHAPTER 9

HOW CAN THIRD PARTY TOOLS BE USED?

Jeff Kuhn and Seann Dikkers

"I don't think I would have ever even tried it without that mod in place. It makes running a server absolutely easy and seamless."

- Minecraft Teacher

"I realized that Minecraft has servers that kids, up to 100 people, could connect to... and so I just started messing around with it and building the world"

- Eric Walker, Designer of World of Humanities.

Adding Possibility

This chapter profiles the more exotic, and jaw-dropping, creations of the larger *Minecraft* community. As teachers, tapping into this community can amplify using the game in the classroom. The wealth of information and expertise in this community shows the scale and possibilities inherent in Minecraft that serves as such an allure to our students. By the end of this chapter you should have a grasp of setting up classroom servers, modifications, importing custom maps, and I have included a quick reference guide to outstanding resources currently available at the end of the chapter.

If you have never spent time playing video games, it's not just the initial excitement that makes them engaging it is the potential - or possibility. I would argue that possibility is more important than excitement, because possibility is the feeling the player puts into the game. Players initially play a game out of curiosity, but they embrace and play a game like Minecraft over time because they have projects, goals, expert achievements, and internalized hopes for the game. After a first exposure to Minecraft, most players look forward to trying new worlds, customizing servers, and import pre-generated worlds; these are possibility spaces. These kinds of customizations allow for the world itself to be part of the story for your learners.

For instance, in Bethesda Softworks' *Skyrim* the land of Skyrim is a character unto itself. Every facet can be explored; the mountains and forests are not just distant backdrops but fully rendered environments brimming with wildlife and brigands. Ubisoft's *Assassin's Creed III* features a historically accurate revolutionary-war era Boston, simmering with rebellion and detail so rich that the window frames of King's Chapel are exact. Both may not be appropriate for classroom use (yet!), but model how powerful a world can be when rich with detail and visual impact. Below you will see how to bring exceptional pre-made worlds into your classroom.

Yet it is not just the worlds that are important to gamers; it is what we can do in those worlds. Great games entice the player to explore. We play games because we want to make a difference in the worlds we choose to inhabit. We want to see the world shaped by our actions and ingenuity; it's why we play. We want to make our mark. When you learn how to import a world, you also learn by default how to use worlds as a student deliverable within your classroom. They can make their mark, tell their story, build their models... and turn it all in!

This chapter explores how we as teachers can 'mine' these dynamic worlds to create new possibility spaces for learning in the classroom. My goal is to present options that increase opportunities for classroom use and provide you language to ask for those things (say, with your technology facilitator), but leave more elaborate tricks, sources, and skills to the often updated internet.

The chapter begins with an overview of how to start using 'seeds', 'maps', and 'mods'. Then, the chapter concludes with a list of maps and worlds by subject areas. Throughout the chapter I have included ideas and suggestions for classroom possibilities for these seeds, maps and mods.

Add Classroom Possibilities with 'Seeds'

Underneath the blocky trees, past the gold ore and diamonds, past the bedrock an algorithm rests, it is what powers *Minecraft* - 'seeds'. When a new map is created, *Minecraft* generates a set of numbers and letters that will determine the characteristics and layout of the new map, the numbers are called a 'seed' and they uniquely identify every map made for Minecraft prior to a player moving the first block.

If you tell me your seed number, I can easily type it in to my Minecraft program and take a look at your map as it was originally generated. For many players this is their first step into a larger world. I will not be able to see what you have built on your map, but I will see your original starting map, so you can share unique landmarks, quirky bugs, or quickly show me how to find diamonds deep below the earth.

Seed trading is one of the first major activities to drive online Minecraft communities. Using seeds is easy, it requires no special modifications to *Minecraft*, and as such make an excellent introduction to using and saving unique maps. Accessing a unique seed is a simple process. Seeds are a great way to get new maps to play but require care; each time the algorithm gets an update the seed will produce another world. Finally, consider taking time to play different maps yourself! New seeds can dramatically change the game experience itself from map to map.

Sharing Your Map's Seed Number

1) Begin by opening up singleplayer Minecraft and create a new world, naming it Seed Test.

2) Once inside the game, press [T].

3) Type '/seed'. Minecraft will reply with your seed number.

4) Copy this seed number, write it down or you can take a screenshot [F2].

Next let's import the seed. First delete our last map named Seed Test, we can recreate the map now that we have the seed.

Importing Another's Map Seed Number

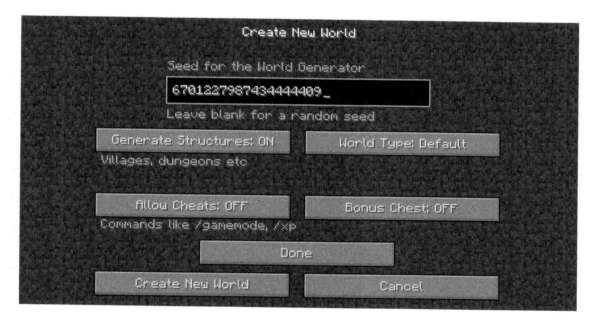

Figure 1: Copy your seed number on the Create New World screen

1) On the 'Select World' screen, select [Create New World].

2) On the 'Create New World' screen select [More World Options].

3) On the More World Options screen input the seed number.[1]

4) You return back to the 'Create New World' page. Enter an original name for this world and you are set to open it up and play.

While seeds are unaltered products of the game itself, maps are player designed. These player maps are what have turned *Minecraft* into a phenomenon[2]. Utilizing the wealth of resources online is a surefire way to get the students invested into your Minecraft classroom.

Classroom Ideas for Using Seeds

- Students can venture into different parts of the world mapping shorelines, mountains ranges, or discovering biomes and the flora and fauna within. Using grid paper your adventurers can create a world map, and because they are using the same seed, they will be able to combine their maps into a whole.

- Provide students a physical paper map with directions to a particular point of interest. Find this location or locations ahead of time and make sure they are far from the starting point (or 'spawn' point) so that they are hard to find without your directions. Challenge students to follow your Minecraft map.

- Use a seed number to provide a particular kind of map to students. This can serve as muse as they experience a specific geography or to write exploration journals in the vein of *The Worst Journey in the World*, by Apsley Cherry-Garrard or *South* by Ernest Shackleton. For example, if your class is reading *South*, you can use a seed that features extensive use of a polar biome.

Simple enough? Simply knowing how to grab a seed number and passing that along to others opens up a few exciting classroom possibilities. Once you get comfortable with that skill, it's time to play with importing maps.

Adding Classroom Possibilities with 'Maps'

Minecraft players can save and share designed worlds commonly referred to as 'maps'.[3] 'Maps' are seeds that have been modified by players or showcase a particular player creation.

---

[1] Changing the [World Type:] variable can interfere with seed generation so leave it as Default.

[2] Great websites to find unique and interesting seeds are: http://www.Minecraftseeds.info/ and http://Minecraft-seeds.net/

[3] Note that 'seeds' are untouched 'maps'. Once you start building and want to show what you've built, you will want to share the 'map', not the 'seed'.

Maps show off projects and world designs that are stunning - and they can be educational. Imagine that instead of just reading about Johnny Tremain, students could tour Boston in 1776.

> "I'll have a room of fifteen computers and half the kids run their own servers. They are typing in each others ip addresses. They are hopping on each other's servers. They are seeing what each other is doing."

Maps range from the simple objects or buildings, like Shakespeare's Globe theater; to larger projects, like a full recreation of *Harry Potter's Hogwarts*, *Tolkein's Middle Earth*, or[4] the *Odyssey's* Grecian World. Look to the end of the chapter, for a list of popular maps by subject area.

Figure 2: 1940s New York recreated block by block

You do not have to build awesome Minecraft settings, you can import them. The community around *Minecraft* is teeming with shared maps.

As a side note, make sure you properly cite your source - especially when you use it in class. Mapmakers encourage fans to share maps under the condition that the mapmaker is given proper credit. As Shirky (2010) describes, in *Cognitive Surplus*, failure to give credit is *the* crime of online communities. The use of any map in *Minecraft* is the result of a mapmaker's labor, and therefore they deserve credit for their amazing work and this is a chance to model digital ethics to your students.

---

[4] A great source for *Minecraft* maps is Planet *Minecraft*: www.planet*Minecraft*.com/

Minecraft community etiquette also asks that if parts or structures of a map are integrated, a 'sign' indicating the creator of the structure should be placed outside the main entrance within your world. Any student should be able to walk up to your *Parthenon*, for instance, and see who built it.

Installing Maps

Installing a few single player maps is great practice before moving onto custom maps. It has a slight intimidation factor at first but once the basic system is understood you'll be able to install any map you want. Maps are easily imported into *Minecraft* but the route differs slightly for PCs and Macs - we'll cover each.

First, you will need a data file to import. You can download these from community sites (bundled as a compressed, or .zip, file), or you can pull that file from your system if you want to share a world you have built.

#	WINDOWS OS	APPLE OS
1	Press the [Start] button.	Click anywhere on your desktop.
2	Type [%appdata%], in the 'Search' field.	Select the [Go] menu at the top of the screen, then [Go to folder...].
3	Double click the folder "Roaming\.minecraft\saves" [5]	Type [~/Library/Application Support/Minecraft].
4	You are in the "Saves" folder. (To share maps, share any of these folders)	Find the "Saves" folder. (To share maps, share any of these folders)
5	To add maps, drag and drop into this folder.	To add maps, drag and drop into this folder.

This folder, once located, is your local information for each world you have played in. In *Minecraft* terms, this means that all of your buildings and designs are in these data files. When you share this folder, other players can see all you have done at the point you shared it. When you add another's world folder[6] to this file, you will be able to see their work.

Installing maps works well if you are operating with single player accounts and maps on unique computers.

---

[5] If the search results do not return "Roaming\.minecraft\saves", double-click the "Roaming" folder and look for it there.

[6] Note that these are data files, not .exe files. You should never have to 'run' a program for this task.

Installing Maps... on a Multiplayer Server

Once the maps have been downloaded for single player installing them onto a multiplayer server is simple. First, if you pull a 'map' folder from online, you may have the luxury of handing that over to your organization's 'tech person'. (In fact, in many school settings, that person may not want you even loading *Minecraft* onto the school computers!)

"I'm blessed with an IT staff that is open and excited about this stuff."

This should get you started and enable you to set up a server for multiple players to see an imported 'map' together.

1) Find the map folder for the world you would like to install and download it to your desktop.
2) See the last section to open your *Minecraft* folder. Instead of "saves", look for a file called "server". Open it.
3) Find the "saves" folder here and move the map folder here.

Next we need to associate that map folder to the server. To do that we need to adjust the server properties.

1) Open the server properties file by right click on the file and select 'Open with' either Notepad on PC or TextEdit on Mac. This file controls the behavior of the server and can be used to change to fundamental properties of the server game.
2) In the server properties file, find the **level-name=**, which should be the fifth line of the list.

```
#Minecraft server properties
#Mon Aug 05 11:20:51 EDT 2013
generator-settings=
allow-nether=true
level-name=world
```

Figure 3: Mastering the server file opens new game possibilities

3) Type the name of the new map after the = with no space. It is critical that the name inserted into this line matches the name of the new map exactly, so it is best to copy/paste the name.

With the above instructions you be able to switch worlds on your server quickly depending on the subject matter of your class. For a list of worlds that you can bring to the classroom see the end of this chapter. Running a vanilla server can accommodate almost all classroom activities, but we may want to add a little panache to our world and for that we need modifications.

Classroom Ideas for Using Maps

Custom maps are a fast-track option for the classroom and can be incredibly useful when targeting a specific learning opportunity. We can use maps to place the students in scenarios or situations that foster particular skill sets.

- Explore the streets of an ancient Roman city as part of a history class, or recreate the adventures of Lewis and Clark in a blocky replica of frontier America - both available in the maps at the end of this chapter.

- Create redstone circuits to power an algorithmic logic board or to fabricate machinery such as railcars and mining equipment. The game mechanics that students must manipulate in these scenarios are the same mechanics used in simple programming.

- A class studying genetics can use dye to color sheep then breed them to study mendelian inheritance. As the sheep breed their color traits are passed to their offspring - certain colors are recessive while others are dominant 'genes'.

- Investigate the complex systems of supply, demand and resource management in a sustainability class by using Dr. Short's Tragedy of the Commons map at the end of the chapter

- Students reading *Harry Potter* can wander the halls of Hogwarts or engage in a Hunger Games scenario to bolster in an after school reading club.

Adding Classroom Possibilities with Mods

'Mods', or modifications, allow players to add options, new game rules, alter game content, modify the textures (appearance), or give players added abilities. Basically, you can add a mod to alter the core programming of the software - so they broadly can do almost anything to the game, but tend to be smaller changes that lend themselves to player, or classroom, preferences. For example in my writing class students experience the zombie apocalypse. I used mods to change 'skins' (the appearance of the player) of the creatures and made the creatures immune to daylight.

Some modifications have become large enough that they utilize their own launcher, which has simplicity issues for us as teachers and server hosts.

Some mods incorporate elements of other video games such as the *Portalcraft* mod. Others are just for fun - the *Natural Disasters* mod integrates random earthquakes and volcanic eruptions in a *Minecraft* map. Mods such as *Bukkit* are designed to streamline the creating and managing of servers and most single-player modifications have a server counterpart.

While not extensively covered in this chapter I overview the leading modification systems that exist outside of the official *Minecraft* game. Namely, I will review the major mod managers: 1) MinecraftEDU, 2) Bukkit, and 3) Forge. Any of which are well established and easy to use.

MinecraftEDU

Joel Levin has made an excellent *Minecraft* mod specifically for classroom use called *MinecraftEDU*. Over time it has expanded into a wide range of customs packs that has nearly turned *Minecraft* into entirely new games.

> "We have a large number of building tools that make it easier for teachers to get their content in the game...we put in a large number of tools for ease of use to create structures and buildings or whatever. We have the server which is dead simple to use."

Features:

- Pre-installed tools manage that students' movements and building abilities to create focused learning situations.

- Unique teacher tools such as information blocks, freezing student movement, and the ability to assign homework in game.

- Access to support material that includes lesson plans and curricular goals

- Included server tools that enable quick server installation and management.

Bukkit

The Bukkit pack is a set of server management tools designed to make the installation and use of *Minecraft* modifications easy for server managers. Over time it has expanded into a wide range of customs packs that has nearly turned *Minecraft* into entirely new games.

Classroom mods:

- MC MMO - This mod takes *Minecraft* into the realm of role-playing games such as *World of Warcraft* and *Final Fantasy*. It adds XP systems, party systems for group play, and thirteen skill sets that players can use to level-up. Altering this mod to make those skills sets reflect 21st century skills for the classroom would be a huge boost to classroom teaching.

- Multiverse – This staggering mod allows server hosts to create a series of interconnected worlds that can each be configured for unique configurations, biomes and even creature spawning.

Forge

Forge allows for installing and maintaining modifications in both single player and server games of Minecraft. It's widespread use and simple interface has made it a popular choice for modders and is a great choice for the classroom.

Classroom mods:

- MCA – Minecraft Comes Alive breathes new life into the game's generic villagers. The mod provides new skins, customizable dialogue and conversation trees for the villagers to better integrate them into the play experience.
- Buildcraft - This mod includes machines that can be constructed to dig for resources and build structures. A great mod for teaching engineering.
- Chisel - This mod is just one example of the many mods that incorporate decorative blocks to increase the level of design and customization of buildings.

We have tested seeds, saved maps and learned a mod or two. Getting comfortable with these functions in *Minecraft* takes practice and time, but doing it is great experiential learning. Keep in mind that *Minecraft* is very forgiving of mistakes so if you seem to have placed too many items in the wrong place, you can delete your entire Minecraft folder and start fresh. Each time *Minecraft* is initialized from scratch it will generate all the needed files and folders in the '.minecraft' folder. As you experiment with maps and mods never be afraid to start anew and give it another go.

Finally, there is an incredible community of teachers, players and programmers out there willing to help those truly lost so be sure to seek help as needed. As this chapter is dated, those communities will not. They will continue to post new ideas, videos, and connect people figuring out how to use not just Minecraft, but the next new thing too. Even remarkable teachers pointed out that connecting was key to their learning. For instance, World of Humanities builder Eric Walker:

> "I first looked at videos of what people were doing like um, Steven Elford... who'd been using it for science purposes in the classroom and Joel Levin, himself, who has been using it in the classroom in his technology classes"

Get online, look at some videos, meet some new people, and start with a few of the suggestions above. Seeds, maps, and servers are more of a 'stage 2' skill level, but you will do fine if you just approach it step by step and with a few online friends.

A Possibility List

Here they are, the maps. Each personally tested and played, these maps represent the wealth of resources available for the *Minecraft* teacher. The maps are organized by teaching context and from there listed alphabetically. All maps feature a download link and where possible a link to further information. Each map features teaching suggestions.

Social Studies

World of Humanities – Eric Walker
An educational map of immense scale, Eric's World of Humanities map has developed over time into a full scale RPG adventure where students can interact with characters and complete quests in a social studies-based narrative. While the rest of the maps all have specific content tied to them with World of Humanities that is almost impossible. In Eric's magnum opus students can study history, social science, cultures, geography, economics; if you can find it in a school curriculum you can find it in World of Humanities!
https://dl.dropboxusercontent.com/u/53773950/World of Humanities/minecraftEdu - World of Humanities - May2013beta.zip

Minecraft Denmark - Danish Geodata Agency
Denmark has taken it as a source of pride to become the first country to be recreated at a 1:1 scale inside Minecraft - in Minecraft scale one block = one meter. Designed to get students interested in spatial data, the designers encourage players to explore the country and build a home of their own. The maps is a great choice for classes on geography, history and language arts. How long will it be before we see a language arts class create a Hamlet machinima? Currently the map exists on a server but can be downloaded - yet be warned it weighs in at a whopping 1TB.
http://download.kortforsyningen.dk/content/danmarks-frie-geodata-i-minecraftverden

Oakland Minecraft – The Museum of Art and Digital Entertainment
Even if you do not live in Oakland, this incredible map is less about what it is than how it was built. A faithful recreation of Oakland California, it is unique in that the builders were solicited from the news-aggregator website Reddit. The map builders were not from Oakland but used Google Maps and other online sources to recreate the city. Teaching the kids spatial thinking and skills? Have them examine a city via Google Earth and then build for accuracy in Minecraft. Imagine a messy classroom with students huddled around computers, sheets of butcher paper and chalkboard sketches as they build Chicago.
https://www.dropbox.com/sh/y1i3nr9o0pqyzxu/y_meOs4EDi/Oakland04.26.13.zip
website: http://www.themade.org/node/184

Project Zearth – Xoyjaz
This sprawling map feature five major cities and several villages spread throughout the world connected by road and rail. This map weighs in at an impressive 461MB but in it students could be separated into city groups to examine common core standards of competing beliefs and goals, methods of engagement, and conflict and cooperation. A great option is to place different classes into different cities and teach the topics of movement, region and human settlement. Create a disaster in one city; forcing the students to migrate into cities controlled by other classes could be a powerful way to teach the high school world geography course standards.
http://www.planetMinecraft.com/project/zeon-city/

Roman Domus – WLhokies
A map of a fictional city of ancient Rome that strives for historical accuracy. The map features details such as impluviums, household shrines, and tablinum. Students studying Roman history could establish a Senate to run the city while the teacher – or clever student - instigates civil war, then bring peace through the exercise of new consolidated powers and the class can experience the fall of the Roman Republic and the rise of the Roman Empire.
http://www.planetminecraft.com/project/roman-domus---historically-accurate-world-save-schematics/

Project America Map – Blake
The continental U.S. is rendered into block form in this expansive map. Largely undeveloped, this map could be used for exploration, geography lessons or even a simulation of the Oregon Trail. Students can replicate the frontier lifestyle of early America or even run a simulation of the founding of America. After a few hours of playing this map my students began to call for rules and codes of conduct. While it's great to teach civic participation, when it derives naturally from student play it is epic learning.
http://dudeguy.com/mceworlds/worldfiles/ProjectAmericaMap.zip

The Tourist – Stratocrafteur

This adventure map features four hours of content set in the Montmartre district in the north of Paris. True to its real-life counterpart, this map centers on the Sacré-Cœur basilica and replicates the streets of Paris to a remarkable degree. Students could use the map to create walking tours of Paris or explore the streets and journal what they find or using French to demonstrate the Common Core call for language and cultural understanding through create using of resources.

http://www.planetminecraft.com/project/adventure-map-the-tourist/

The Zone (Chernobyl Exclusion Zone) – tsarcorp

70% complete at the time of this writing, the map replicates Pripyat, Ukraine, the city abandoned in 1986 days after the Chernobyl disaster. A city which has been largely isolated since. Combined with readings on the events leading up to the disaster, students could draft first person essays on what they had to abandon as they evacuate the Chernobyl exclusion zone. Combine this map with the the Uranium Mod modification and high school students studying scientific inquiry and application could investigate the city to uncover what caused the mass exodus. Gamer Pro Tip: Students may recognize this map as Pripyat as the city was featured in the popular game *Call of Duty 4: Modern Warfare*.

https://mega.co.nz/#!U5cECaQR!Ygu1kT3jvis5aqyyR36XxxTirN5BFA8GF1Gy3RnYdJs
website: http://tariqsarwar.net/zonecraft/

Tragedy of the Commons - Dan Short

In this map players experience the depletion of shared resources and how to promote sustainability through co-operation. Dr. Short's places players in a glass dome with a limited number of trees to harvest as resources. Round one of the scenario seeks to educated players on the dangers of the tragedy of the commons while round two encourages players to develop strategies to prevent the depletion of resources. Common core standards to explore in this map include writing standards that demonstrate student ability to state an opinion in writing on the issue presented and support that opinion with structures in which related ideas are grouped to support the writer's purpose. This map is excellent for the Common Cores topic of sustainability.

http://faculty.rmu.edu/~short/research/minecraft/MC-Tragedy-Commons-v2.zip

United States Capitol Building - Senator Aubin

This replica of the Capitol Building can help students develop the inflated self-interests of Congressional members. Students can practice core topics of roles and systems in the heart of the U.S. government. While this map is an excellent external replica the inside of the building is largely unfinished and so requires a little prep time.

http://www.mediafire.com/download/u50npq5664o07w6/Famous_Buildings.zip

Vertoak City - fish95

Vertoak is a city-themed adventure map for *Minecraft*. All the buildings are fully furnished with hidden secrets and treasures. City maps like this one can be populated with villagers that will then begin to craft materials and trade with student players. Students can also begin to mine and craft resources to develop an economy to explore issues of resource scarcity and economic response to scarcity. Thriving city-style maps are excellent tools to explore economic decision-making, understand the issues of costs and benefits, and investigate economic alternatives.

http://www.Minecraftmaps.com/creation-maps/vertoak-city/viewdownload

Math and Science

Skyblock – Noobcrew

A classic map that has been downloaded over 5 million times, Skyblock features one tree, 20 blocks of dirt and a chest containing two items. What you do and how you survive is up to you. This is a great map to generate divergent thinking and problem solving skills.

https://dl.dropbox.com/s/ye1mist5lgpda0y/SkyBlock1.1.zip?dl=1

Survival Island Map – Ashien

Similar to the famous Skyblock, this map come with rules and challenges to increase the challenge level. Build a wheat farm, ten bookcases and a cobblestone generator all without leaving the island. Puzzle maps are excellent tools to generate communication and collaboration among students as they work through problems of spatial thinking and mathematical problem solving.

http://www.mediafire.com/download/zca5iu3vpgmuv2u/SurvivalIslandv1.zip

Environmental Sampling – Dr. Dan Short

Dr. Short has created a series of interesting single-focus maps. This one focuses on methods scientists use to sample for pollutants. Besides making maps, Dr. Short has some great resources and a paper on using Minecraft in the science classroom. You can find more on his website, so be sure to check it out.

http://faculty.rmu.edu/~short/research/minecraft/MC-Env-Sampling.zip
website: http://faculty.rmu.edu/~short/research/minecraft/

The Periodic Table of the Elements – Dr. Dan Short

This particular map showcases a massive periodic table of the elements. The map does a great job of relating real-world elements to *Minecraft* resources such as copper and redstone. Yet not all the elements feature descriptors, leavings science students ample opportunity to fill in the blanks. This map is a great way for students to learn to define and classify minerals and called for in the Earth and Space Science strand of the standards.

http://faculty.rmu.edu/~short/research/minecraft/MC-Periodic-Table.zip

Writing

Globe Theater – GSACommando
Explore the home of Shakespeare's plays in this historical map. Combined with custom skins and machinima players of this map can stage and record the Bard's plays. For teachers unfamiliar with it, Machinima is the creation of movies using the real-time graphics of video games. *Minecraft* players have produced some phenomenal examples of machinima and developed considerable 21st century skills in the process. Staging a machinima version of a Shakespeare play would involve planning, collaboration, scripting, storyboarding, digital costuming, filming, editing and post-production. In the process they would have extended exposure to one of the greatest writings in English history.
http://www.mediafire.com/download/egphma029p15gpd/GlobeTheatre.zip

Kingdom of the Sky – Blame the Controller
Kingdom of the Sky is unique as it uses Youtube to create a voice over narration to the map. Designed as an adventure map, the world is perfect for exploring or questing. Use this map for some experiential learning fun before students develop written narratives focused on details and clearly structured events as called for in the Common Core.
http://www.mediafire.com/download/3uhwsves4em49ll/KotSv14.zip

PotterCraft – Musicdudez
This map aims to recreate Hogwarts and contains Hogsmeade, Diagon Alley, Ministry of Magic, and the Malfoy and Wesley residences. A creative literature class could use the map to inspire students to write fan fiction in the Potter universe.
http://www.mediafire.com/download/ht4vmjbjmw3t7ht/PotterCraft+Pre-Release+1.zip
website: http://www.planetMinecraft.com/project/pottercraft---the-wizarding-world-of-harry-potter-in-Minecraft/

Crafting Azeroth - Rumsey
The entirety of *World of Warcraft's* land of Azeroth is featured in this truly epic 24 GB map. While the team continues to work on Outland and Northrend, the Eastern Kingdoms and Kalimdor are available in the download. The map features enormous cities and expansive wilderness. Students can use the medieval backdrop for learning the 21st century skill of communication and collaboration as they build in-game communities.
http://www.minecraftforum.net/topic/997352-crafting-azeroth/

Herobrine's Mansion - Hypixel
This map is an example of the work of Hypixel, whom many consider to be one of the best Minecraft mappers. This is a map all teachers should explore as this is what our students do for fun after school. Hypixel has created many great maps and developed online fame as a result. It is cognitive surplus and the digital world at its finest and a fun map to boot.
http://hypixel.net/threads/herobrines-mansion-adventure-map.200/

Lord of the Rings Mod
The Lord of the Rings is an in-progress build of J.R.R. Tolkien's Middle Earth. This will include content from J.R.R.Tolkien's most famous work, the *Lord of the Rings* series, and eventually other related tales such as the Hobbit and the *Silmarillion*. Currently the mod is still in the early stages of development, but a new public beta download is released approximately every month. An after school fantasy book club could use the map to trace the travels of Bilbo and Frodo or create new adventures for their own Middle Earth characters. http://lotrminecraftmod.wikispaces.com/home

WesterosCraft
This massive server is an active process of replicating George R.R. Martin's *A Song of Ice and Fire* land of Westeros. The server currently allows visitors with no build access and parts of the map are available for download – King's Landing, The Dreadfort and Winterfell at the time of this writing. An incredible example of the skillsets players bring to *Minecraft*, this server requires players seeking to help build the Westeros map must submit an application including examples of previous builds. The map of Winterfell could be used for K-8 social studies projects exploring the concept of feudalism and the resulting social systems. http://westeroscraft.com/home

Bio

Jeff Kuhn is a writing instructor and technology consultant at Ohio University. Each semester Kuhn teaches a first year writing class using *Minecraft*. He has presented widely on the use of video games in higher education, specifically in the field of language acquisition. He has taught English as a second language in Japan and served as a teacher trainer in Peace Corps Mongolia. Since 2011, Kuhn has created a series of contextualized learning classes where students use *Minecraft* to experience events that serve as the foundation for writing journals. His current project is "Journaling the Zombie Apocalypse". In class students read selections of Max Brooks' *World War Z* and *The Zombie Survival Guide* while playing a modified version of *Minecraft* that replicates a zombie invasion. The project ends with students devising a zombie preparedness plan for the city of Athens, OH using what they learned playing *Minecraft*. Kuhn also worked on the U.S. Department of State's *Trace Effects*, a video game designed to engage students in English language learning. He is currently pursuing his PhD in Instructional Technology advised by Dr. Seann Dikkers.

CHAPTER 10

USING GAME-BASED APPROACHES TO INCREASE LEVEL OF ENGAGEMENT IN RESEARCH AND EDUCATION

Joseph C. Toscano[1], Andrés Buxó-Lugo[1,2], and Duane G. Watson[1,2]

"Minecraft is coming into different venues than what we thought was possible"

- Carl Manneh, Mojang, Co-founder and Managing Director

And Now for Something Completely Different

[A note from the editor...]

What you are about to read is a bit of a departure from the rest of the book. So far each chapter has focused on some element of teacher appropriation or evaluation of Minecraft. In the following pages, the authors have generously volunteered to publish their research as as a chapter in this book. Normally this kind of piece would be found in a journal and it will read as such. That said, the authors provide us glimpse of the range of impact Minecraft has in other fields, and I believe opens up an exciting host of possibilities for classroom use of Minecraft as a tool for action research, scientific method, and data collection. In that light, though different, this chapter fits perfectly.

[1] Beckman Institute for Advanced Science and Technology, University of Illinois at Urbana-Champaign
[2] Department of Psychology, University of Illinois at Urbana-Champaign

Using game-based approaches to increase level of engagement in research and education

Abstract

Improving student engagement in the classroom has the potential to increase academic success. Similarly, increasing participant engagement in experiments may allow researchers us to better study behavior. As a result, both educators and researchers would like to have tasks and activities that are interesting and engaging, and game-based approaches have been proposed as one way to achieve this goal. We describe a paradigm based on Minecraft that we have been using for basic research in psycholinguistics, the study of the cognitive processes underlying language use. This approach provides us with a task that is interesting for participants, elicits naturalistic language, and allows us to run controlled lab experiments. Moreover, it demonstrates that level of engagement can have large effects on behavior. This illustrates how platforms like Minecraft can provide us with a useful new tool for creating studies that are more engaging, allowing us to examine research questions that we have not been able to address using other techniques.

Context

Many researchers have argued that more engaged students show better learning outcomes (Skinner & Belmont, 1993; Finn & Rock, 1997; Marks, 2000), and as a result, teachers want to ensure that students remain engaged in the classroom. Level of engagement also plays a role in basic research: laboratory experiments are often needed to address certain questions, but these studies typically lack the naturalness of real-world environments and abstract away from many details (Clarke, 1997; Wertsch, 1998). This can make the experiment much less engaging, and it can unintentionally change participants' behavior (Orne, 1962). Thus, a major challenge for both researchers and teachers is to find ways for participants and students to be highly engaged.

Several approaches for increasing student engagement, in particular, the use of technology in classrooms (Kulik & Kulik, 1991) and game-based approaches to teaching and learning (VanSickle, 1986; Moeller, Cootey, & McAllister, 2006), have been proposed. Though debate about the effectiveness of some techniques continues (see Randel, Morris, Wetzel, & Whitehill, 1992, and Vogel, Vogel, Cannon-Bowers, Bowers, Muse & Wright, 2006, for reviews), previous work has shown that game-based approaches can increase engagement and lead to better learning outcomes (Squire, 2003; Barab, Thomas, Dodge, Carteaux, & Tuzun, 2005). Given this, we were interested in whether game-based tasks also provide a way to increase participant engagement in the lab.

To test this, we developed a platform for running experiments using Minecraft (see Chapter 2). Our research focuses on language use, and we used the game to create an experimental task that is more interesting and engaging than those that are typically used in our field. Often, in lab-based studies, participants do not use natural language—for example, their speech lacks the typical prosody (details below) we see in real-world conversations. This creates a challenge for researchers who, on the one hand, are interested in studying natural language, and on the other, need to have the precise experimental control offered by a laboratory setting. Game-based tasks provide a potential solution to this problem, and as we show here, they allow us to create conditions where participants are more likely to use natural language (i.e., they produce speech that is more characteristic of everyday language use).

This study is not about Minecraft, per se, but rather, it provides an illustration of how Minecraft (and games like it) can be used as a tool for research (on language use, or on other topics), allowing us to study cognitive processes that we could not examine using typical laboratory approaches. Although our study did not focus specifically on learning, it may provide insights for educators who want to increase student engagement using similar approaches, as well as ideas for researchers that struggle with engaging study participants.

In the following sections, we discuss 'level of engagement' as it pertains to education and research in cognitive science, with a particular emphasis on our own field of psycholinguistics, the study of how humans produce and understand language. Then, we describe our game-based task to illustrate how it allows us to run controlled experiments in the lab, while creating an environment that affords natural language use. Our study highlights how games like Minecraft provide a platform for achieving higher degrees of engagement in the laboratory, and more generally, how game-based approaches give us a tool for studying phenomena that we would not have been able to study any other way.

A Discussion on Validity in Psychological Research

One reason we are particularly interested in game-based approaches is that they can provide experimental control, and simultaneously, allow for more natural behavior. This allows us to study a variety of cognitive processes usings tasks that participants find interesting. Similarly, one way that teachers might increase student engagement is to make learning environments richer and more stimulating. Indeed, the environment can affect learning in a number of ways, and many researchers have discussed the importance of context on learning outcomes (e.g., Brown, Collins, & Duguid, 1989). This ties into the idea of studying phenomena in situ, in the way they occur in the real world, something that has been advocated by researchers in a number of fields (Clark, 1997; Hutchins, 1995), including education (Brown et al., 1989; Halverson & Clifford, 2006; Squire & Dikkers, 2012). Although the research questions we focus on here require studies in the lab, game-based approaches, in general, may also give us measures that more closely reflect behavior outside the lab.

The challenge faced by researchers is that it is often difficult to design studies that are constrained enough to give us experimental control, yet flexible enough that they reflect complex, real-world conditions. This is a general issue with trying to maximize the validity of a study—the extent to which we can draw valid conclusions from it—since different aspects of the study allow for different types of validity. For example, internal validity refers to the extent to which the results are not explained by other factors, something that is typically achieved via the precise control offered by lab experiments. Contrast this with external validity: the extent to which results generalize to other situations, something that is typically achieved through fieldwork and studies in real-world environments.

Internal and external validity are opposed to each other such that changes to a study that increase one tend to decrease the other. As a result, there is no "perfect" experiment that can completely maximize both. However, it is possible to find a balance between the two. Game-based approaches, in particular, provide a way to do this, since they allow us to create controlled virtual environments that afford more natural behavior than what we see in typical lab settings. These issues apply to research studies in a number of fields, and they have been particularly relevant in psycholinguistics. Research in this area spans a range of topics, from understanding how listeners recognize speech, to understanding how sentence structure is interpreted during reading, to understanding the representations and processes that underlie discourse and conversation.

A great deal of psycholinguistic research has used laboratory experiments. However, language produced in the lab can differ from real-world language in a number of ways. For example, conversational speech depends on a collaborative effort between interlocutors that take one another's perspective and goals into account (Schober & Clark, 1989; Hanna, Tanenhaus, & Trueswell, 2003; Nadig & Sedivy, 2002; but also see Keysar, Lin, & Barr, 2003; Yoon, Koh, & Brown-Schmidt, 2012), but speakers' goals may be very different in the real world than they are in a constrained lab experiment. In a conversational setting, speakers are generally motivated to be appropriately informative, since their communication has real-world consequences. On the other hand, in a laboratory setting they might be more motivated to simply accomplish the task quickly.

Given this, we need experiments that allow for natural language use in the lab. Virtual environments provide a platform that may allow us to achieve this goal. Part of the appeal of a sandbox-type game (like Minecraft), in particular, is that it allows us to quickly develop complex environments with minimal programming.

A number of previous studies have used various types of virtual environments to study cognitive processes. Virtual reality has been used to investigate phenomena ranging from visual and tactile perception (Atkins, Jacobs, & Knill, 2003) to the ability to detect changes in the environment (Triesch, Ballard, Hayhoe, & Sullivan, 2003). Game-based approaches, in particular, have been used to study processes like selective visual attention (Green & Bavlier,

2003). Other researchers have explored language use in virtual environments: Steinkuehler (2003), for example, describes how multiplayer online games can provide a tool for studying language. Together, these results suggest that virtual environments may offer a viable platform for studying cognition in a way that allows for more participant engagement. As we describe below, we found that they do.

Using a Computer Game for Research

We developed a technique using Minecraft (Persson & Bergensten, 2011)–specifically, a customized version for education called MinecraftEdu (Koivisto, Levin, & Postari, 2012)– to accommodate the need for greater participant engagement in our experiments. The goal was to create a richer environment and more interesting task, while still allowing us to address the research questions we were interested in. The game provides a platform for doing this, since it gives us an immersive environment that can be precisely controlled. Specifically, in our study, Minecraft provides a context in which we can observe particular aspects of language use.

We used this approach to investigate how certain characteristics of *prosody* are used in conversational speech (see Buxó-Lugo, Toscano, & Watson, submitted, for more details). Prosody includes several aspects of language that describe *how* words are produced (as opposed to *what* the words are), including properties like word stress and rhythm. For example, the statement "We're going to the store *now*?" is heard as a question when the talker's fundamental frequency (roughly corresponding to the pitch of her voice) rises for the word *now*, whereas the same sequence of words, "We're going to the store now.", is heard as a statement when it does not.

In Buxó-Lugo et al., we investigate how talkers convey information about *discourse status* in a conversation by making certain words prosodically prominent (i.e., emphasizing them). Discourse status refers to whether particular information is new in a conversation or has been mentioned previously. For example, a talker might say "Give me the *red* one", emphasizing the word *red* to contrast it with some other color or to indicate that they are referring to a new item that has not been mentioned previously in the conversation.

We were interested in which acoustic cues talkers use to convey discourse status in conversations. That is, how does the speech signal change when a talker wants to indicate to their partner that a particular piece of information in the conversation is new? Answering this question is important, not only for understanding the processes underlying language production and comprehension, but also for developing computer systems that take discourse status into account when recognizing speech.

Previous work has suggested that there are a number of acoustic cues that the talker might use and that listeners might take advantage of in interpreting discourse status (Wagner &

Watson, 2010). These include word duration (talkers tend to indicate new information by making words longer), intensity (discourse-new information tends to be perceived as louder), and different aspects of the talker's fundamental frequency (discourse-new information tends to be produced with higher fundamental frequencies). However, previous studies that have used typical laboratory tasks have found inconsistent effects when measuring these cues. Thus, it seems as though talkers do not reliably convey discourse status, and as a consequence, we might conclude that listeners would not be able to infer information about prosody in a conversation.

Our goal was to see whether this was really the case, or whether talkers simply do not produce realistic language in typical lab-based tasks. Specifically, we were interested in whether talkers would convey discourse status more reliably if the task was more engaging, making it more akin to natural conversation. Indeed, studies analyzing spontaneous speech, which lacks the control needed to satisfy internal validity, have found that talkers use these cues to a certain extent, though there has been disagreement about which cues provide the most information (Kochanski, Grabe, Coleman, & Rosner, 2005; Kim, Yoon, Cole, & Hasegawa-Johnson, 2006). Nonetheless, with more natural tasks, talkers may more reliably convey discourse status information to a conversational partner.

Experiment Design and Results

The experiment consisted of two tasks. One was a picture description task, in which participants saw sequences of colored squares on a computer display, and they were asked to read the sequence aloud from left to right (e.g., *"red, black, pink"*). Then, they saw another set of colors that was either (1) identical to the first, (2) a completely different set of colors, or (3) a set where only the second color changed (e.g., *"red, **green**, pink"*). This allows us to manipulate the discourse status of specific words (i.e., whether they were repeated or not) and measure the acoustic properties of the words to see which cues (if any) talkers use to convey differences in discourse status. This task is typical of those commonly used in lab experiments studying prosody.

We contrasted this with a second task using Minecraft. We created a Minecraft world in which two participants had to work together to cooperatively solve puzzles. The two "players" were seated in physically different rooms and communicated through headsets. The world was designed so that the players proceeded sequentially through a series of rooms, each of which contained a puzzle that they needed to solve. Each room had a locked door, and after solving the puzzle, the door would open, allowing the participants to proceed to the next room.

Participants were given a brief (5-10 minute) introduction to the game and a tutorial on how to control their character and interact with the environment. Then, they completed a series of 36 puzzles in the game. They had as much time as they needed to complete each puzzle, and they continued until they reached the end or had been playing for one hour. Half of the puzzles (18 trials; 9 unique puzzles) served as fillers meant to keep the game interesting. To solve them, one participant generally had information that they needed to provide to their partner.

Figure 1 shows an example of one of these puzzles. Here, the two participants have to work together to move a block to a particular location. Pressing the colored buttons on the wall will move the block in different directions. In this case, the participant has to tell their partner to press the *blue*, *pink*, and *yellow* buttons in sequence to move the block to the correct location. After they do this, the door will open and they can proceed to the next puzzle. Other filler trials included games where participants needed to complete a maze, fire an arrow at a target, or guide a minecart to a particular location. Critically, each of these puzzles needed to be solved cooperatively by having the participants exchange information with each other, creating situations that allowed for natural conversation.

Figure 1. Example of a puzzle in the experiment from one of the participant's perspectives. The other participant's character (labeled as Player 1) can be seen in the top center of the figure.

The critical experimental trials consisted of puzzles where we manipulated the information status of specific words in the discourse, just as we did in the picture description task. These took the form of "combination locks" in which one player was given a code (a set of colors) and the other player needed to enter it in the correct sequence to unlock the door and exit the room. This allowed us to create trials in the game that corresponded to those in the more typical (but less interesting) picture description task described above.

Figure 2 provides an example of one of the "combination lock" trials. The two participants' characters are located in different rooms and cannot see each other. The participant on the left (Player 1) sees the sequence of *red, black,* and *pink* blocks on the wall. Her partner (Player 2) sees a set of colored buttons on his wall. To solve the puzzle and open the door, Player 1 tells her partner the first sequence ("red, black, pink"). After Player 2 presses those buttons in the correct order, a new set of colors appears on the wall in Player 1's room. She gives this new sequence to her partner (*"red, **green**, pink"*) who presses the corresponding buttons, solving the puzzle and triggering the doors to open. Both players then move on to the next puzzle.

Importantly, we varied the color sequences in the same way as in the picture description task. The same colors, color sequences, and trial orders were used in both tasks. Thus, the only thing that differed was the task itself, where one task led to low levels of engagement (picture description), and the other was much more interesting (the Minecraft task).

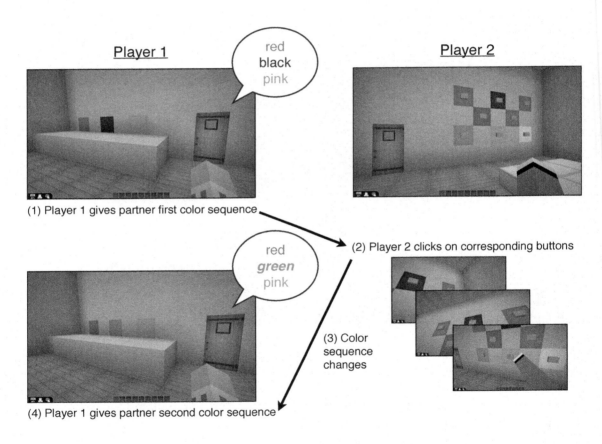

Figure 2. Example of the sequence of events for one of the "combination lock" (discourse status) puzzles in the experiment.

The transcript below illustrates a typical exchange between two participants in the Minecraft task on a trial in which the colors were different for each sequence (making all the colors in the second sequence new to the discourse):

> Player 1: Ok, now my order is **black**, **red**, and umm, **blue**.
> Player 2: Ok.
> [The color sequence changes for Player 1.]
> P1: Ok, now, I have **white**, **brown**, and **green**.
> P2: Ok.
> [The door to the room opens after Player 2 enters the second sequence.]
> P1: Ok, off we go!

Here, we are interested in how the participants emphasize the second set of colors to distinguish it acoustically from the first set (e.g., the acoustic differences between the word *brown* in the example above and the word *brown* spoken on a trial in which that color was repeated).

Twenty-four pairs of participants were given the Minecraft task, and another 24 were given the picture description task. We found that in the (more typical) picture description task, participants did not provide very reliable information about discourse status. In contrast, in the Minecraft task, participants provided information to their partner using a number of acoustic cues. For example, differences in duration between discourse-new and discourse-given words were larger in the Minecraft task (98 ms) than in the picture description task (30 ms; see Buxó-Lugo et al. for details about the results). Thus, talkers provided more information about the discourse status of these words in the game.

These results demonstrate that level of engagement matters. By providing participants with a more interesting task, language use was more natural, and we were able to measure properties of spoken language that we could not measure using typical laboratory approaches.

Discussion and Application

The game-based task provided us with the balance we needed in the experiment: it was constrained enough that we expected participants to say particular words (allowing us to make the necessary acoustic measurements) but unconstrained enough that participants engaged in natural conversations about the game. Although our task isn't completely free of any constraints (since participants are still instructed to solve the puzzles in the game), it offers them much more flexibility. This allows us to have control over the stimuli and conditions, but gives participants a more natural, and importantly, a more engaging task. The study described above represents a middle-ground between more typical laboratory experiments and analyses of real-world language that have no experimental control, satisfying (to some degree) the demands of both internal and external validity.

How do these results inform educational research and the utility of game-based approaches? The current example provides preliminary evidence that more engaging environments can have large effects on behavior, since we found that talkers provide information about prosody more reliably in the game-based task than in the less interesting picture description task. Given this, and the observation that level of engagement is related to student performance (Skinner & Belmont, 1993; Finn & Rock, 1997; Marks, 2000), similar approaches might translate to a variety of settings in education. For instance, our study could be used in a science class to teach students how to design an experiment: it illustrates concepts such as experimental control, independent and dependent variables, and randomization. The game provides a concrete way to teach students about these ideas, and this may make them more memorable.

Many of the other advantages that this approach provides, such as ease of use and flexibility for a variety of tasks, may also be useful for teachers (Table 1). As we have shown here, computer game approaches provide researchers with a tool for increasing participant engagement, which in turn, allows us to study basic cognitive processes. For teachers, increasing the level of student engagement is, in itself, beneficial and may lead to better learning outcomes.

Table 1. Game-based approaches in research and classroom settings.

	LABORATORY RESEARCH	CLASSROOM USE
Level of engagement	Higher	Higher
Environment	Richer stimuli	More stimulating learning context
Ease of use	High	High
Effects	More naturalistic behavior	Improved learning
Flexibility/Adaptability	Can be used to study a range of cognitive processes	Can be used for a range of subjects

The results of the experiment also mirror work in education on game-based approaches (Squire, 2003; Barab et al., 2005). With respect to questions about language and literacy, previous work has suggested that when students are able to choose topics in a game-based task, they perform at a higher reading level (Steinkuehler, Compton-Lilly, & King, 2010). The Minecraft task used in our experiment may have had a similar effect for us: by allowing participants to choose their topic of conversation within the game, they may have been more engaged and produced more natural language (in contrast to the picture description task, where their speech was much more constrained by asking them to simply read the color sequences).

This approach could be further extended to learning contexts. The experiment itself could provide a useful platform for teaching students about language processing. By participating in the experiment, students can gain a better understanding of the cognitive processes that underlie language production, as well as a better sense of how researchers study these processes.

These types of tasks could also be useful in language learning situations. If they produce a higher level of engagement than other approaches, they could lead to more successful outcomes. For researchers, this paradigm could also be adapted for studying other aspects of language processing, and experiments using this approach could be constructed to study many other cognitive processes (e.g., attention, working memory, executive function). Because of the flexibility of computer-game platforms like Minecraft, a wide range of environments can be constructed that are suited to studying specific phenomena. Thus, many of the same benefits that we have outlined here can be gained by researchers in other fields as well.

To conclude, we have demonstrated that a game-based approach can be used to increase participant engagement in laboratory studies, providing a valuable experimental paradigm for researchers. Thus, games like Minecraft are useful not only as teaching tools, but also for scientific research. They offer a flexible, easy to use platform for increasing level of engagement both inside and outside the classroom, and they open up a number of possibilities for studying behavior in a way that few other techniques can.

References

Atkins, J.E., Jacobs, R.A., & Knill, D.C. (2003). Experience-dependent visual cue recalibration based on discrepancies between visual and haptic percepts. *Vision Research, 43*, 2603-2613.

Barab, S., Thomas, M., Dodge, T., Carteaux, R., & Tuzun, H. (2005). Making learning fun: Quest Atlantis, a game without guns. *Educational Technology, Research, and Development, 53*, 86-107.

Brown, J.S., Collins, A., & Duguid, P. (1989). Situated cognition and the culture of learning. *Educational Researcher, 18*, 32-42.

Buxo-Lugó, A., Toscano, J.C., & Watson D.G. (submitted). Effects of participant engagement on prosodic prominence.

Clark, H.H. (1997). Dogmas of understanding. *Discourse Processes, 23*, 567-598.

Finn, J.D., & Rock, D.A. (1997). Academic success among students at risk for school failure. *Journal of Applied Psychology, 82*, 221-234.

Green, C.S., & Bavelier, D. (2003). Action video game modifies visual selective attention. *Nature, 423*, 534-537.

Halvorson, R.R., & Clifford, M.A. (2006). Evaluation in the wild: A distributed cognition perspective on teacher assessment. *Educational Administration Quarterly, 42*, 578-619.

Hanna, J.E., Tanenhaus, M.K., & Trueswell J.C. (2003). The effects of common ground and perspective on domains of referential interpretation. *Journal of Memory and Language, 49*, 43-61.

Hutchins, E. (1995). *Cognition in the Wild*. Cambridge, MA: MIT Press.

Keysar, B., Lin, S., & Barr, D.J. (2003). Limits on theory of mind use in adults. *Cognition, 89*, 25-41.

Kim, H., Yoon, T., Cole, J., & Hasegawa-Johnson, M. (2006). Acoustic differentiation of L- and L-L% in switchboard and radio news speech. In R. Hoffman & H. Mixdorff (Eds.) *Proceedings of the Third International Conference on Speech Prosody 2006*, Dresden, Germany.

Kochanski, G., Grabe, E., Coleman, J., & Rosner, B. (2005). Loudness predicts prominence: Fundamental frequency lends little. *Journal of the Acoustical Society of America, 118*, 1038-1054.

Koivisto, S., Levin, J., & Postari, A. (2012). MinecraftEdu [computer software]. Joensuu, Finland: Teacher Gaming.

Kulik, C.C., & Kulik, J.A. (1991). Effectiveness of computer-based instruction: An updated analysis. *Computers in Human Behavior, 7*, 75-94.

Marks, H.M. (2000). Student engagement in instructional activity: Patterns in the elementary, middle, and high school years. *American Educational Research Journal, 37*, 153-184.

Moeller, R.M., Cootey, J.L., & McAllister, K.S. (2006). "The perpatos could not have looked like that," and other educational outcomes from student game design. In B.E. Shelton & D.A. Wiley (Eds.), *Educational Design & Use of Computer Simulation Games* (pp. 129-152). Rotterdam: Sense Publishers.

Nadig, A.S., & Sedivy, J.C. (2002). Evidence of perspective-taking constraints in children's on-line reference resolution. *Psychological Science, 13,* 329-336.

Orne, M.T. (1962). On the social psychology of the psychological experiment: With particular reference to demand characteristics and their implications. *American Psychologist, 17,* 776-783.

Persson, M., & Bergensten, J. (2011). Minecraft [computer software]. Stockholm: Mojang.

Randel, J.M., Morris, B.A., Wetzel, C.D., & Whitehill, B.V. (1992). The effectiveness of games for educational purposes: A review of recent research. *Simulation Gaming, 23,* 261-276.

Schober, M.F., & Clark, H.H. (1989). Understanding by addressees and overhearers. *Cognitive Psychology, 21,* 211-232.

Skinner, E.A., & Belmont, M.J. (1993). Motivation in the classroom: Reciprocal effects of teacher behavior and student engagement across the school year. *Journal of Educational Psychology, 85,* 571-581.

Squire, K. (2003). Video games in education. International *Journal of Intelligent Simulations and Gaming, 2.*

Squire, K., & Dikkers, S. (2012). Amplifications of learning: Use of mobile media devices among youth. *Convergence, 18,* 445-464.

Steinkuehler, C.A. (2003). Massively multiplayer online video gaming as a participation in a discourse. *Mind, Culture, and Activity, 13,* 38-52.

Steinkuehler, C.A., Compton-Lilly, C., & King, E. (2010). Reading in the context of online games. In S. Goldman, J. Pellegrino, K. Gomez, L. Lyons, & J. Radinsky (Eds.), *Proceedings of the 9th International Conference of the Learning Sciences* (pp. 222-229).

Triesch, J., Ballard, D.H., Hayhoe, M.M., & Sullivan, B.T. (2003). What you see is what you need. *Journal of Vision, 3,* 86-94.

VanSickle, R.L. (1986). A quantitative review of research on instructional simulation gaming: A twenty-year perspective. *Theory and Research in Social Education, 14,* 245-264.

Vogel, J.J., Vogel, D.S., Cannon-Bowers, J., Bowers, C.A., Muse, K. & Wright, M. (2006). Computer gaming and interactive simulations for learning A meta-analysis. *Journal of Educational Computing Research, 34,* 229-243.

Wagner, M., & Watson, D.G. (2010). Experimental and theoretical advances in prosody: A review. *Language and Cognitive Processes, 25,* 905-945.

Wertsch, J.V. (1998). *Mind as Action.* New York: Oxford University Press.

Yoon, S.O., Koh, S., & Brown-Schmidt, S. (2012). Influence of perspective and goals on reference production in conversation. *Psychonomic Bulletin and Review, 19,* 699-707.

CLOSING

The effort by myself and many others to better understand teaching and learning with new media technologies is still ongoing. Even the focus on Minecraft will change by the time of this publication and imitators/improvers will have already released new and exciting versions of sandbox style, build anything, design spaces for players. However, I suggest that the fine art of Teachercraft will remain the center of how we can apply of these new opportunities for teaching and learning. Teachers will continue to become aware of, validate, experiment, appropriate, and iterate on classroom lessons. They will continue in refining and assessing new media learning each and every school day. If we want to improve schools, we need to likewise see and study these amazing teachers and share their practices widely. We need to study exemplary teaching with new media technology in order to train and support effective practice.

In Teachercraft, I have attempted to identify not only how to use a particular game, but how teachers learn about and design new learning opportunities for their students. Where we attempted to pack the outstanding ideas within the chapters also, this book is essentially an extended research on formative data from a collection of exemplary educators. At its best, the intent is to create and build on a conversation about how teachers go about their own learning.

Gaming media is a vibrant space for thousands of classroom supplements, activities, design tools, and can inspire vocabulary and lesson design to be more playful in general. If the patterns identified here hold true across digital media appropriation, then it may be the case that our traditional models of lecture-based professional development (PD) are simply not as applicable to how our innovative teachers actually learn for themselves. As delighted as I am with the work in this book, I'm actually even more excited about what this can mean for the design of professional development for teachers that have not yet learned about Minecraft, or any other digital gaming for amplifying their classrooms. What if these patterns could inform school wide PD programming? What if digital mediation of information simply can be learned more easily using the patterns found in this book? What if Teachercrafters are actually waiting in the majority of our teachers, we just haven't yet shown them how to do it? Much more needs to be explored to see if these findings are generalizable to other digital tools, other topics, and other learning spaces.

Finally, I do hope this work has encouraged you to share, try, and tune into ongoing development of Minecraft and mainstream game designs in general. As you try and innovate yourself, please seek myself or any of these authors out and share what you are working on. You never know, your story may end up in a book like this some day.

- Seann

Lightning Source UK Ltd.
Milton Keynes UK
UKOW04f0707130916

282876UK00011B/263/P